3-D ADVENTURES
AWESOME PLANET

ARCTURUS

ARCTURUS

This edition published in 2011 by Arcturus Publishing Limited
26/27 Bickels Yard, 151–153 Bermondsey Street,
London SE1 3HA

ISBN: 978-1-84858-054-1
CH001936EN

Printed in China

CONTENTS

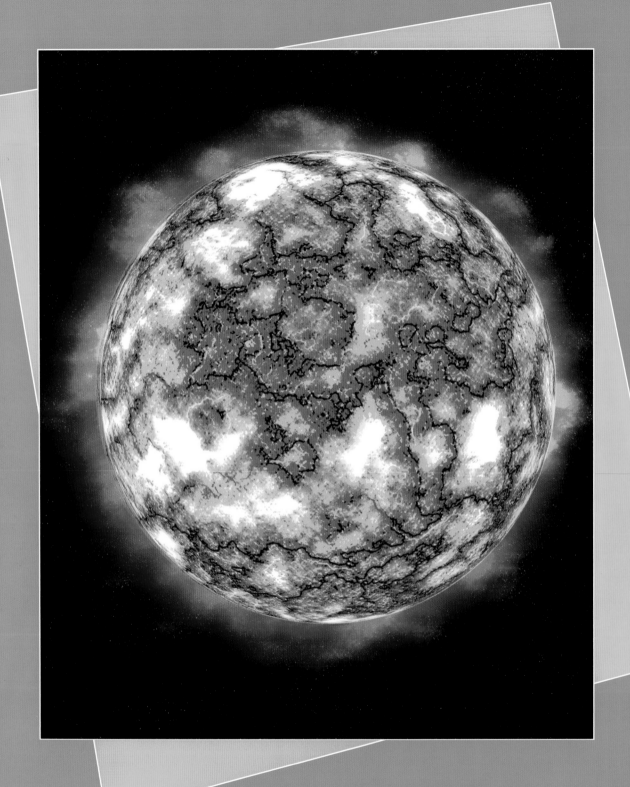

SPACE

IN THE BEGINNING

S pace is all around us and scientists think that it stretches on forever—which can make your head hurt if you think about it for too long. As you'd expect, something that big has a lot of stuff in it. Let's find out where it all came from and what's there.

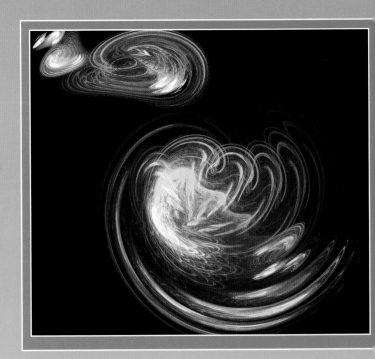

▲ BOOM!

Most scientists believe that the universe began with a bang. Between 10 billion and 15 billion years ago the universe exploded out from a tiny point, hurling out gases that would go on to form the stars and galaxies. This is called the big bang theory and scientists can still pick up an "echo" of radiation from the universe's violent beginning.

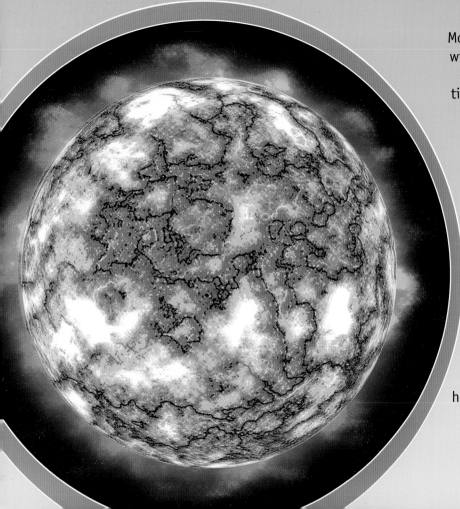

◄ SHINING STAR

Our Sun is just one of the billions of different stars that are out in space. Stars are really just big balls of gas. They come in all sizes and temperatures from cool dwarf stars, to medium ones like our Sun, to huge, hot giants many, many times the size of our Sun. The only reason our Sun looks different to all the other stars is that we're so much closer to it.

◀ THE BIG ONES

A planet is an object over a certain size that orbits, or travels round, a star. There are three main types of planet: planets that are made mainly from rock, like our own; planets that are made mainly from ice, which are generally the smallest planets; and planets made from gas, which are the biggest. A moon, on the other hand, is an object over a certain size that orbits a planet rather than a star—just like our Moon (though the name rather gives that away!).

Scientists believe that the outside of the Sun is about 10,000°F—but that's nothing compared with the center, which is an astonishing 27,000,000°F.

TOO SMALL ▶

Asteroids orbit stars but are too small to be planets, even though they are made from the same kind of stuff as the Earth-like planets. Comets are lumps of ice and dust that also orbit a star. Sometimes you can see these for a few days before they're off again on their journey round the Sun. Meteors are small lumps of rock and iron that fall to Earth—you can sometimes see them streaking across the sky.

OUR NEIGHBORS

S pace is unimaginably large—it is thought to go on forever—but it can be broken down into local neighborhoods. Ours is called the solar system and makes up a tiny part of a galaxy called the Milky Way, which itself is only a tiny part of the universe.

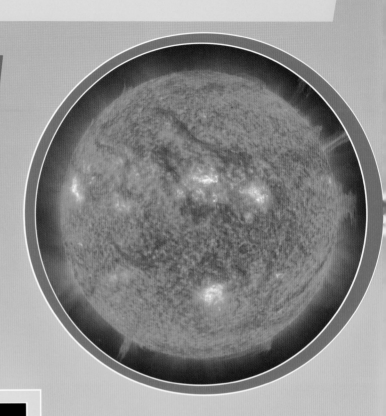

▲ AT THE CENTER

At the heart of our solar system is the Sun, and it is the Sun's gravitational pull that keeps the planets circling around it rather than shooting off into space. Scientists believe the Sun could be up to five billion years old and that it will still be around for another five billion years. The Sun, although hugely important to us, is actually only a medium-sized star, and is one of many billions of stars in the universe.

◄ THE MOON

At around 235,000 miles away, our nearest neighbor is the Moon. Many scientists believe that the Moon used to be part of the Earth, but it broke away when our planet was being formed. However, our Moon is not the only moon in the solar system—some other planets have them too. Jupiter, for example, has sixty-two moons.

▶ ROCKY PLACE

It's not just planets that orbit the Sun; there are thousands of smaller rocks, called asteroids, which are held in place by the Sun's gravitational pull. Most asteroids can be found in a group called the asteroid belt, which lies between Mars and Jupiter. So far, scientists have spotted over 90,000 of them there.

▼ TO BE OR NOT TO BE?

You might think it is very easy to tell what is and what isn't a planet. For many years it was thought that our solar system had nine planets: Mercury, Venus, Earth, Mars, Jupiter, Saturn, Uranus, Neptune, and Pluto. However, in 1996 the idea of what made up a planet changed and Pluto was reclassified as a dwarf planet. There have been two other dwarf planets spotted so far and there may be many more.

Comets are balls of ice and dust that have wide orbits around the Sun—some take as long as thirty million years to go round once!

9

SUPERSTARS

T he most obvious elements of the night sky are the stars. But these are not just simple points of light—there's much more going on up there than you think.

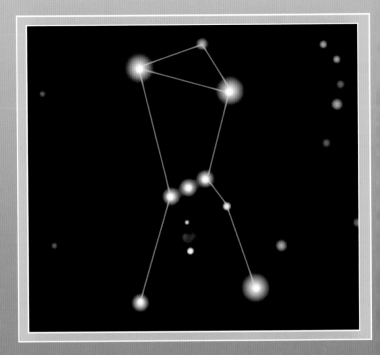

▼ GANGING UP

Although stars seem to be randomly dotted around the night sky, they all belong to groups called galaxies. No one knows how many galaxies there are, but there could well be as many as 200 billion. Our own galaxy is called the Milky Way and contains anywhere between 200 billion and 400 billion stars. It gets its odd name from the milky white line of stars that you can see if you're well away from built-up areas.

▲ SKY PICTURES

When our ancestors looked at the stars way back in the mists of time, they drew imaginary lines between some of them to make pictures. We call these pictures "constellations." There are eighty-eight different constellations, including this one, Orion the Hunter. Either our ancestors were terrible at drawing or they had very good imaginations, as constellations never look much like what they are supposed to be. However, they can be a handy way of navigating and, in the time before GPS handsets or even maps, they were very useful.

STAR FACTORY ▶

If you have a telescope you may be able
to see stars being born. There are huge
clouds of gas and dust in space called
nebulae and these are the universe's star
factories. Within a nebula, smaller clumps
of gas and dust sometimes start to spin
around one another. As they spin they
get hotter and faster and closer together.
Eventually they spin out of the nebula
and become fully fledged stars. Sounds
like an easier way of giving birth than
humans have managed!

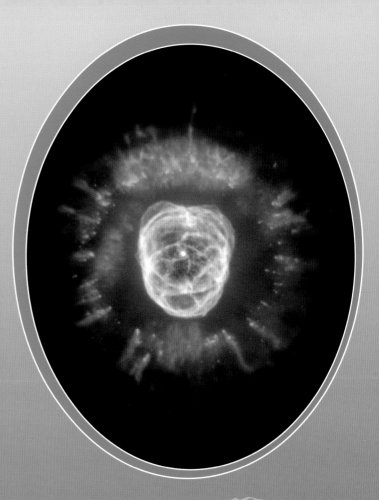

Galaxies
come in three basic
shapes: spiral (like a
pinwheel), elliptical
(like an oval), and
the all-purpose
irregular.

◀ SUPERNOVAS

Stars don't last forever, unfortunately. As a
general rule of thumb, the bigger the star the
shorter its life will be. However, no matter how
big it is, stars always end the same way—in a
huge explosion called a supernova! Don't worry,
though—our Sun isn't predicted to do this for
another five billion years. Although a supernova
is the end for one star, it's the beginning for
new ones as the material that's thrown out by
the explosion is used in the creation of brand-
new stars.

SPACE-WATCHING

F rom the very dawn of the human race, people have found the stars fascinating. As time progressed, so did our ways of looking toward the skies. Our enthusiasm for looking at space has remained undimmed to this day.

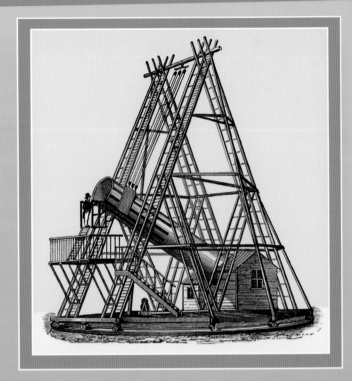

▼ OBSERVING THE STARS

The telescopes used by professional space-watchers, or astronomers as they are known, are housed in special buildings called observatories. Generally, observatories are found at the tops of hills in sunny climates. That's not so astronomers can get a good view of the countryside while topping up their tans—it's so they can get a good look at the stars. High up, there is less interference from pollution in the atmosphere and if the country is sunny there's going to be less cloud to get in the way.

▲ FIRST GLANCE

Until the invention of the telescope in the early 1600s, people used their naked eyes to see the stars. That was fine as far as it went, but even the most basic of early telescopes was an improvement. The first telescopes allowed people to see the craters on the Moon for the first time and even some of the moons around Jupiter.

HUBBLE BUBBLE ▶

We all know that if you're closer to something you're likely to get a better view of it. Astronomers used that logic when they launched the Hubble Telescope into space in 1990. Not only is this telescope closer to the stars, it will also never be affected by pollution and cloud cover. Although it might look like a fat drainpipe covered in aluminum foil with a couple of solar panels stuck to it, the Hubble has sent back pictures from space that the ancients would never have dreamed of, including the birth of stars.

Instead of using one huge telescope, astronomers often use lots of smaller telescopes pointing at the same bit of the sky.

LISTEN UP ▶

Studying space isn't just about looking at the stars—it involves listening to the universe as well. Objects that are too far away to be seen can sometimes be heard—so long as you've got the right equipment. Radio telescopes look a bit like the satellite receiver dishes you get on homes, only much, much bigger. The largest one is the Arecibo telescope in Puerto Rico, which is a huge 1,000 feet in diameter. Objects such as stars emit radio waves and this is what radio telescopes such as the Arecibo look for.

MYSTERIES

As you might expect from something as big and as generally far away as space, there are lots of things that scientists don't know or even understand. Here are some of the big ideas and mysteries.

WHIRLPOOLS IN SPACE ▶

One of the scariest things in space is a black hole. These are incredibly dense parts of space whose gravitational pull works a little like a whirlpool, dragging everything that gets too close into its center. The pull is so strong that even light itself can't escape it. Some scientists believe that black holes occur when giant stars die—and that there might even be a hole at the center of our own galaxy!

◀ INTO THE TUNNEL

One interesting idea that scientists have is that there might be tunnels in space leading to different parts of the universe—or even back in time! These tunnels are known as "wormholes," and are based on the theory that a person could travel through a black hole and, instead of being crushed at its center, could pop out of another hole instead. Scientists know that gravity can affect time (a difficult idea, we know), so theoretically it's possible. We don't have the means to test it yet, but you probably wouldn't like to be the one who tried it first.

SOMETHING MISSING ▶

Although space has got lots of things in it, like stars, planets, and other stuff, scientists think that over 80 percent of space has stuff in it that they can't figure out. It has a gravitational force but there doesn't seem to be anything there. Confused? So are the scientists. They call this missing bit of space "dark matter," and they have no way of detecting what it is because it doesn't give off light or radiation.

The Pioneer 10 space probe had a plaque attached to it with drawings of where it had come from and who sent it, just in case any aliens found it.

◀ WE COME IN PEACE

Are there little green men alive on other planets or are we alone in the universe? Well, many scientists believe that there are living things out there—but they probably don't go around in flying saucers. Instead, they might be tiny, basic micro-organisms that can withstand intense heat or cold. Presently, scientists think there's a good chance there may be this type of life on Mars, Venus, or even on the Moon.

15

ARE WE ALONE?

The question of whether we are alone in the universe has bothered people for centuries. On one hand, the universe is so large that it would seem unlikely that Earth is the only planet with life; but on the other hand, there has been no firm evidence of life existing elsewhere—yet.

Every television and radio broadcast ever made filters into space, so somewhere an alien could be watching our old TV programs.

▼ PROBES

Over the last 40 years scientists have sent messages into space. Two *Pioneer* space probes as well as the *Voyager* probes each carried plaques with pictorial messages showing who we are and where we come from. This worries some scientists, as we can't be sure that an alien who finds one will be friendly. However, the chance of anyone—friendly or not—finding them is very small.

CANALS ►

In the late 1800s an Italian astronomer called Schiaparelli was studying Mars and reported that he saw something that looked like channels, which was translated into English as "canals." As canals are man-made, this implied that there had been, or still was, life on Mars. They turned out to be optical illusions caused by the atmosphere around both planets. This is also true of the supposed "face" that appears in the Cydonia region of the red planet.

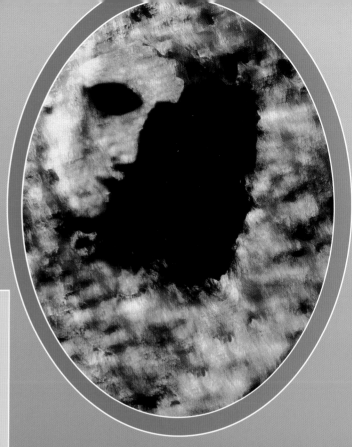

◄ LIKELY SPOT

Scientists believe that planets need to be just the right distance from a star for them to have any chance of supporting life; too near and conditions are too hot, too far away and it's too cold. Rocky planets like Earth are a good place to start looking, but trying to find such a planet is very difficult—they are so far away that we can't see them properly! Astronomers are still looking though.

LISTENING IN ►

The gigantic Arecibo radio telescope in Puerto Rico is usually trained to listen to the stars, but occasionally it listens out for evidence that aliens might be sending us messages. It went one stage further in 1974, when a short message was beamed out to space toward a cluster of stars in the constellation Hercules. We haven't had a call back yet, but that's because it's going to take over 24,000 years for the message to arrive.

SOLAR SYSTEM

HOME SWEET HOME

I f someone asked where you live, you'd probably give your street address. But you could answer that question in a way that every living thing on Earth or on any of the other seven planets could, too. We all live in the solar system.

▲ AROUND THE SUN

Greek astronomer Aristarchus (ca. 310–230 BC) was the first person to claim that the Earth revolves around the Sun. However, Polish astronomer Nicolaus Copernicus (1473–1543), above, usually gets the credit. Few people believed Copernicus's theory in his lifetime. It wasn't until German astronomer Johannes Kepler (1571–1630) showed that planetary motions best fit the Sun-centered nature of the solar system that the idea began to gain acceptance.

◄ THE SOLAR SYSTEM

At the center of our solar system is the Sun, a medium-sized star called a yellow dwarf. Earth and the other planets orbit, or travel, around the Sun. Each planet also spins on its axis, an imaginary line through the center of the planet, like a top. Besides the Sun and planets, the solar system also includes moons, meteoroids, asteroids, and comets.

The Milky Way is called a barred spiral galaxy because its spiral arms wind out from a "bar" of thick material at the center.

GALAXIES GALORE

All the stars in the night sky that we can see from Earth are in the Milky Way. However, there are about 50 billion galaxies in the universe, some much bigger than the Milky Way. There are stars in all of them, and who knows, maybe one of those stars is the sun for another planet with life like Earth's.

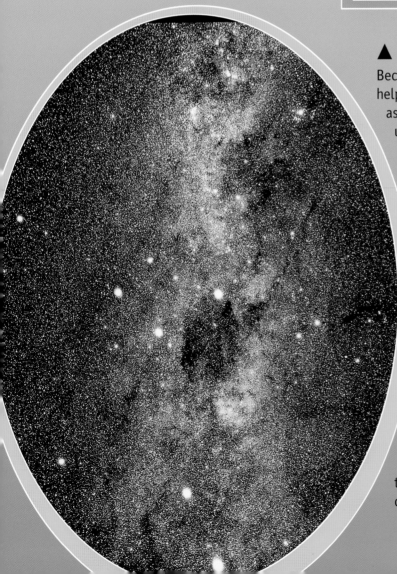

▲ LIGHT-YEARS AWAY

Because the universe is so big, it's not always helpful to measure distance in space the same way as on Earth. Instead of miles, astronomers often use light-years. Light is the fastest type of energy in the universe. A light-year is the distance light travels in one Earth year— 5.9 trillion miles! The Andromeda galaxy (above), the closest spiral galaxy to ours, is 2.2 million light-years away.

◀ THE MILKY WAY

Our solar system is part of the Milky Way galaxy. A galaxy is a cluster of hundreds of billions of stars, plus dust, different types of gas, and empty space. From Earth, the Milky Way appears as a soft glowing band of light encircling the sky. It got its name in ancient times when people thought it looked like a stream of milk in the night sky.

OUR STAR

Hot news! Even on the coldest night in the coldest winter in Antarctica, the Sun is giving heat. Life on Earth could not exist without the Sun, even when you don't see it or feel it.

▼ ONE AMONG MANY

Our Sun is a star, a giant sphere of swirling, burning gases (mostly hydrogen and helium). Because it's the closest star to Earth, it gets a lot of attention. However, every twinkling dot in the sky is another star, some much bigger than our Sun. But our Sun is pretty big in its own right—about 865,000 miles wide. Over one million Earths could fit inside it.

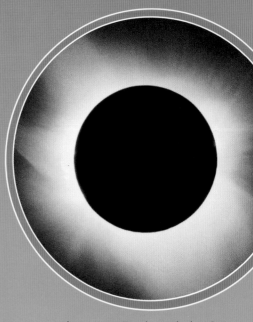

▶ SOLAR ECLIPSE

When the Moon passes between Earth and the Sun, it casts a shadow that passes over a small part of Earth, creating a solar eclipse. In a total solar eclipse you can't see the Sun; you're in the darkest part of the shadow and it will feel like night. If you can still see part of the Sun, you're experiencing a partial solar eclipse. An annular eclipse is when you can see a ring of Sun around the black disk of the Moon. Eclipses usually last about 3 minutes and not longer than 7 minutes, 40 seconds. Before science explained eclipses, some people thought a monster was devouring the Sun!

On August 11, 1999, people from England to India were plunged into temporary darkness during a total solar eclipse that lasted around two minutes. They were lucky to see it! Some countries will have to wait about 80 years before another total eclipse comes along.

GAS, GAS, AND MORE GAS ▶

Three distinct layers of gas cover the Sun. The photosphere is its surface—and is what we can see at any time. The chromosphere is the glowing layer of gas that extends several thousand miles above the photosphere. The corona is the outermost part of the Sun's atmosphere. Its edge is about 10 million miles out from the Sun. Both the chromosphere and the corona are visible to the naked eye only during total solar eclipses.

▶ A DAZZLING DISPLAY

The Sun puts on enormous fireworks shows all the time. Solar flares are short bursts of light from the chromosphere that reach into the corona. Solar prominences (right) are stringy gas clouds that extend from the photosphere into the corona and can last several weeks. Dark blotches on the Sun's surface, called sunspots (above, top right), are places where the gas is cooler. A single sunspot can be larger than Earth.

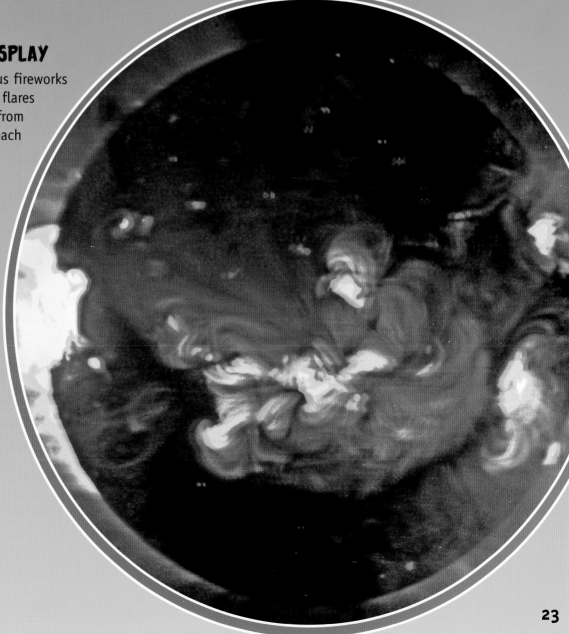

A FAMILIAR PAIR

T he only places in the solar system where humans have walked are Earth and its Moon. No one knows for sure how the Moon was formed. Some believe a large comet or asteroid slammed into Earth. The debris formed a ring around Earth that stuck together to make the Moon.

▲ THE HOSPITABLE PLANET

Earth is the third planet from the Sun, and is just the right distance for living organisms to have enough—but not too much—heat and light to live. There are very hot and cold areas on Earth, but on the whole our planet is very habitable. Location is everything. Venus, one stop closer to the Sun, is too hot, while Mars, one stop farther from the Sun, is too cold. The temperature on Earth is just right for water to be liquid.

◄ WATERY WONDER

Oceans of water cover over 70 percent of our planet's surface. Earth is the only planet with oceans of liquid water, though some other planets and some moons may have liquid water beneath their icy surfaces. It was in this ocean that life first began on Earth. Now our planet is home to billions and billions of living things found nowhere else in the solar system and, possibly, the universe.

◀ A GIANT STEP

In 1969, as commander of the *Apollo 11* mission, Neil Armstrong (born 1930) of Ohio became the first person to set foot on the Moon. Only eleven other men have done the same, during the course of six more Apollo missions. The last one was in 1972. Each mission had a three-man crew, but each time only two got the chance to walk on the Moon. The third stayed in the orbiting ship.

The Moon may have ice mixed in with soil at its poles. Even if there is water on the Moon, it still could not support life because it has no atmosphere. Temperatures on the Moon range from 261°F at noon to -279°F just before daybreak.

▼ PHASES OF THE MOON

The Moon never looks the same as it did the day before, because it goes through phases every month, from crescent (sliver) to quarter moon to full moon to new moon (which looks like no moon). Of course, the Moon doesn't actually change shape; just our view of it does. The Moon has no light of its own—what we see as moonlight is a reflection of the Sun's light shining on the Moon. As the Moon orbits Earth, we see more and more (or less and less) of its bright face.

GOOD NEIGHBORS

E arth and its three closest neighbors—Mercury, Venus, and Mars—are called terrestrial planets because they are similar in size and made largely of rock. But beyond those two facts, Earth and its near neighbors are quite different from one another.

▲ VISIT TO MARS

In 1976, two unmanned probes, *Viking 1* and *Viking 2*, landed on Mars to search for signs of life. They found none. *Viking 2* sent back the above image of the planet's red, rock-strewn landscape. Mars is also home to the solar system's tallest mountain, Olympus Mons, an extinct volcano fifteen times taller than Mount Everest.

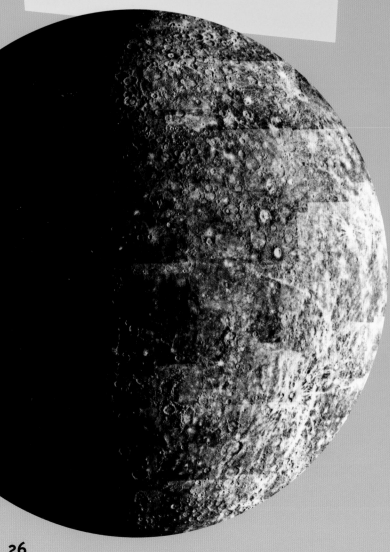

◄ MERCURY

At a distance of 36 million miles, Mercury is the closest planet to the Sun. It is the smallest planet, and has no moons. Mercury has the biggest temperature range of all planets, from -297°F at night to 845°F during the day! One Mercury day equals fifty-nine Earth days (meaning it takes Mercury fifty-nine Earth days to rotate once on its axis). Mercury's landscape is covered with craters and was photographed and researched by the unmanned space probe *Mariner 10* in 1974 and 1975.

◄ MARS

Scientists hope to land humans on Mars, the fourth planet from the Sun, within your lifetime. The Mars day is about half an hour longer than an Earth day, but its year lasts 687 days. Its atmosphere is mostly carbon dioxide, with little oxygen and a high level of radiation. There are also frequent dust storms. Mars has two moons and is about half the size of Earth. Its red color comes from iron in its soil. In other words, Mars is rusty, as well as harsh.

▼ VENUS

Venus is the second planet from the Sun and is the brightest object in the sky after the Sun and Moon. It can often be seen just after dark or at dawn and is also called the "evening star" or "morning star." Venus is the hottest planet in the solar system—with temperatures as high as 895°F. Not only does it rotate from east to west, which means the Sun rises in the west and sets in the east, but its year is shorter than its day! This means it travels around the Sun quicker than it rotates once on its axis. Venus has a string of volcanoes along its equator, including Maat Mons (below). None are known to be active.

Is there life on Mars? Most likely not. Has there ever been? Possibly. Small markings that look like fossilized bacteria have been found on a very old rock believed to be from Mars.

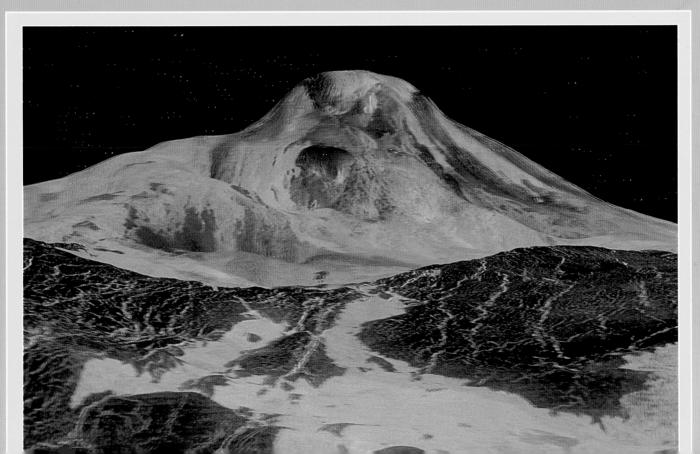

THE GAS GIANTS

T he solar system's powerhouse pair are Jupiter and Saturn. Jupiter is the biggest planet, with Saturn a close second. Like the next two planets from the Sun, Uranus and Neptune, they are made of gases (primarily hydrogen in metallic and liquid form) with cores of rock or rock and ice. All four of these gas giants—not just Saturn—have rings!

▶ MOONS

Eighteen named moons revolve around Jupiter, almost as if it is the center of a solar system of its own. It may have even more moons waiting to be located. In 1610, the Italian astronomer Galileo Galilei (1564–1642) discovered four of Jupiter's moons: Callisto, Europa, Ganymede, and Io. Each can be seen from Earth with binoculars. Europa is covered with surface ice under which may be an ocean of liquid water—and that ocean may contain life. Io (above) is the only other place in the solar system besides Earth known to have active volcanoes.

◀ JUPITER

Jupiter is the fifth planet from the Sun. Its day is only about ten hours long. In fact, it spins so fast that it bulges at its equator. The Great Red Spot, a red swirling circle seen on Jupiter, is a storm over 8,500 miles wide and 16,000 miles long—big enough to cover two Earths! Jupiter itself is 1,300 times larger than Earth. As if a constant storm isn't stressful enough, fragments of Comet Shoemaker-Levy 9 bombarded the planet in an exciting six-day event in 1994. One collision produced an eruption 100,000 times more powerful than the largest nuclear bomb ever detonated.

SATURN ▶

If you think Jupiter's eighteen moons are a lot, Saturn has twenty, and possibly many more not yet discovered. Like Jupiter, Saturn spins very fast. Lasting 10 hours, 39 minutes, its day is a little longer than Jupiter's, but still less than half as long as Earth's. Like Earth, Saturn has auroras in the polar regions (right), which extend about 2,000 miles above the clouds. Saturn's average density is less than that of water, so it would float if you dropped it into a big enough ocean or pool.

In 1989, the space shuttle Atlantis launched the tiny Galileo mini probe. Six years later, Galileo entered Jupiter's atmosphere and sent back data for eight hours before it vaporized. Thanks to this brave little probe, we now know more about Jupiter.

▼ SEEING TRIPLE

Saturn is the sixth planet from the Sun but is almost twice as far away from the Sun as Jupiter. When Galileo first observed Saturn in 1610, he thought he was seeing three planets. Through Galileo's telescope, Saturn's rings looked like two other planets on either side of Saturn. In 1659, Dutch astronomer Christiaan Huygens (1629–1695) confirmed that it was actually one planet with rings. The rings are made of ice, frozen gas, and rock. The rings are not solid—you can see stars through them. Scientists estimate that the rings are at most one mile thick.

DISTANT RELATIVES

T he outermost objects in the solar system—Neptune and Uranus, plus the dwarf planets Pluto and Eris—are a mixed bunch. Neptune and Uranus are similar to Jupiter and Saturn, while Pluto and Eris are smaller than our Moon. They're all very far away, and much of what we know about them was learned only recently.

▶ URANUS

Uranus is the third-largest planet in the solar system, the seventh from the Sun, and four times as large as Earth. It has fifteen named moons and eleven rings (right). Uranus is twice as far from the Sun as Saturn, so when German astronomer William Herschel (1738–1822) accidentally discovered it in 1781, it doubled the size of our solar system! In 1978, another startling discovery was made—like Saturn, Uranus has rings, also made of dust, rocks, and ice. However, they are thin and dark and harder to see than Saturn's.

We are still finding out about what's at the edge of our solar system. Pluto, discovered in 1930, was classified as the outermost planet, but as recently as 2003, another dwarf planet, Eris, was discovered beyond Pluto.

TWO POLES TO THE SUN

Much else that we know about Uranus was not learned until 1986, when *Voyager 2* passed by. Its atmosphere is made mostly of hydrogen and methane. Since it is so far from the Sun, it is also very cold. The average temperature is just -353°F. Perhaps Uranus's oddest feature is that it is sideways! Unlike Earth, its north and south poles face the Sun. When one Uranus pole faces the Sun, the other pole is in complete darkness for half a Uranus year—forty-two Earth years!

TRITON

The large south polar cap on Neptune's largest moon, Triton (far right), is thought to consist of a slowly evaporating layer of nitrogen ice.

NEPTUNE ▶

Neptune, the eighth planet, is a billion miles from Uranus. It was named after the Roman god of the sea because of its rich blue hue. However, it is not water but methane gas that gives Neptune its color. Neptune is not only cold (average temperature is -364°F) but windy, too. Winds whip around the planet at 1,500 miles per hour—the fastest in the solar system. *Voyager 2* discovered six of Neptune's eight named moons and its rings. Although Neptune is usually the eighth planet, sometimes Pluto's orbit crosses inside Neptune's and Neptune is farthest from the Sun. Pluto was closer to the Sun than Neptune from 1979 until 1999.

▼PLUTO AND ERIS

Because it is so small and its orbit is so irregular, Pluto was recently reclassified as a dwarf planet. Pluto is named after the Roman god of the underworld, and its only moon, Charon, is named after the character in Roman mythology who took souls by boat to Hades. In 2003, another object was discovered at the very farthest reaches of our solar system. Although it is bigger than Pluto, the new planet is still only a dwarf planet. At first it was known only as UB313, but in August 2006 it was officially given a name: Eris. Eris is the name of the goddess of chaos and strife in Greek mythology.

ROCKETING ROCKS

Planets, moons, and stars have many smaller companions in space: asteroids, comets, and meteoroids. They are the rock stars of space, but let's hope they never have a greatest hit.

▼ ASTEROIDS

Asteroids are rocky chunks that orbit the Sun. It is estimated that there are a million of them in our solar system, mostly in the belt between Mars and Jupiter. Scientists once thought that asteroids were remains of a planet that exploded. Now most agree that asteroids are fragments that have been around since the formation of our solar system but could not form a planet because nearby Jupiter's gravity was so strong. Most asteroids vary in size from 62 miles wide to 0.6 of a mile. Ceres, the largest asteroid at 580 miles in diameter, was also the first to be discovered.

Many theorize that the dinosaurs were wiped out when an asteroid hit Earth. Such a collision could have sent so much dust into the atmosphere that the Sun's light would have been blocked, thereby killing the plants that dinosaurs ate.

TAIL FIRST

A comet's tail always points away from the Sun, so even when traveling away from the Sun, it shoots tail first. In earlier times, people called comets "hairy stars" and often thought they meant bad luck. In 1995, Comet Hale-Bopp was discovered simultaneously by two American men in different states, and was named after both. It became visible to the naked eye in 1996 and appeared at its brightest in early 1997.

▲ COMETS

Did you know our solar system throws snowballs? They're called comets. A comet is a giant dirty lump of frozen methane, ammonia, and water that orbits the Sun on an elliptical path along the edge of the solar system. Comets have long, luminous tails of gas. Comets originate from a spooky-sounding area called the Oort cloud. In 1950, Dutch astronomer Jan Oort (1900–1992) theorized that a region exists beyond Pluto (and now, Eris) that is a "storage area" for inactive comets.

A LONG WAIT

Halley's Comet, which rockets past Earth every 76 years, is probably the most famous comet. Its discoverer, British astronomer Edmund Halley (1656–1742), was the first to recognize that comets follow the same orbits around the Sun again and again. We can next expect Halley's Comet in 2061. Mark your calendar!

▶ METEOROIDS

Smaller than asteroids but at least as large as a speck of dust, meteoroids are stony or metallic particles that travel through space after breaking off from a celestial body such as an asteroid, comet, or planet. Once they enter Earth's atmosphere, they are called meteors. If they hit Earth, they are called meteorites. Many burn up in Earth's atmosphere, but those that make it to the surface are usually smaller than a fist. On occasion they are bigger, and some have caused damage, but only a few of the approximately one million meteorites that hit Earth each year are even seen. It's much more breathtaking to see the various meteor showers that are visible yearly. The Leonids, for example, put on a show every November.

EXPLORING SPACE

EXPLORATION

If scientists need to get a closer look at space, they send up a spacecraft. There are many different kinds of spacecraft and they are all designed to do specific jobs.

ROUND AND ROUND ▶

Technically, a satellite is any object that orbits a bigger object, but usually the term is used to describe man-made objects. Currently there are around 2,500 satellites in space and they do a variety of jobs, from telecommunications to weather forecasting. The first satellite was launched way back in 1957. It was called *Sputnik* and all it did was send out a simple radio signal so that it could be tracked on its orbit around the Earth. It was pretty basic, but it was the first man-made object to orbit the planet.

◀ A CLOSER LOOK

When scientists want to find out about an object in space, the first thing they do is send out a probe. *New Horizons*, launched in January 2006, was the first probe to orbit the dwarf planet Pluto to provide scientists with unparalleled information from the edge of our solar system. Some probes, such as *Deep Impact*, aren't designed to orbit an object, but to crash into it. *Deep Impact*—or rather a part of it—was sent to crash into a comet called Tempel 1 so that scientists could study what the comet was made of. Understandably, this type of crash is called a "hard landing."

OFF FOR GOOD ▶

Some probes are sent from Earth not to orbit anything or land anywhere, but are fired off into space just to send back information for as long as their batteries can hold out. The probe that is farthest away from Earth is called *Voyager 1*. It was launched in 1977 and is currently around 11 billion miles from the Sun, traveling at a speed of 38,000 miles per hour. It is getting farther away all the time.

There are over 8,000 man-made objects floating around in space, from satellites to old bits of spacecraft and things astronauts have dropped.

▼ WHEELY USEFUL

Not all probes that land on objects in space make a "hard landing." Others land in a more civilized manner and relay their findings back to Earth. More excitingly, some carry rovers with them. Rovers look a little like remote-controlled off-road toys and are designed to drive around the surface of planets. At the moment there are a couple scooting around on Mars, called *Spirit* and *Opportunity*, and they are sending scientists on Earth some fantastic data about the red planet.

TO BOLDLY GO

When the Russians launched *Vostok 1* into orbit in 1961, cosmonaut Yuri Gagarin became the first human to journey into outer space. It was just the beginning of the human adventure in space.

BLAST OFF ▶

The first problem with space exploration is how to get there, which means overcoming Earth's gravity. And to do that you need speed, and lots of it. The only way of getting that kind of speed is by using rockets; the biggest rocket so far was *Saturn V*. This giant stood over 363 feet high and was responsible for sending the first American astronauts into space. Despite its huge size it was incredibly fast, traveling at over 5,250 miles per hour!

◀ ALL IN THE NAME

Well over four hundred people have traveled into space, but only three countries have the technology to get people up there—the United States, Russia, and China. The United States only takes Americans into space, but the Russians will take anyone who can afford to go. And it all depends on who you fly with as to what you'll be called—American and Chinese space travelers are called astronauts, but anyone flying with the Russian space program is called a cosmonaut.

The space shuttle is a space delivery truck—its job is to take satellites into space to launch them and to take scientists and supplies to the International Space Station.

▲ HOME FROM HOME

Getting a human into space is an expensive business, so it makes sense to get your money's worth by keeping them up there for as long as possible. The best way to do this is to build them a home in orbit around the Earth, or a space station as it is called. As its name suggests, the International Space Station is a joint venture between sixteen different countries and is a kind of floating laboratory. At around 240 feet at its widest point, it's also the biggest man-made object in space.

◀ EXPENSIVE RECYCLING

The space shuttle is the first and so far only reusable spacecraft. It is probably also the most complex machine ever built. It can launch itself—with some help from a couple of booster rockets—at over 16,500 miles per hour to get into space and then withstand temperatures of over 1,800°F as it reenters the planet's atmosphere. It also has to make a controlled landing at a specific airfield despite having no fuel left to power its engines. All this comes at a price, though—each shuttle costs around $1.7 billion to build and each mission costs around $450 million!

HUMANS IN SPACE

For many years the only people considered for a space mission—except astronauts—were air force pilots. This is no longer the case, so the people who venture up there require a lot of training and luck to make it out of Earth's atmosphere.

SUPER SUIT ▶

If astronauts have to leave the safety of their spacecraft, the only way they'll survive is if they wear a space suit. A space suit is a complicated piece of clothing that does a number of jobs. It provides oxygen for the astronauts to breathe; it protects them from the temperatures of space and radiation from the Sun, keeps them cool as they work, and allows them to communicate with other people.

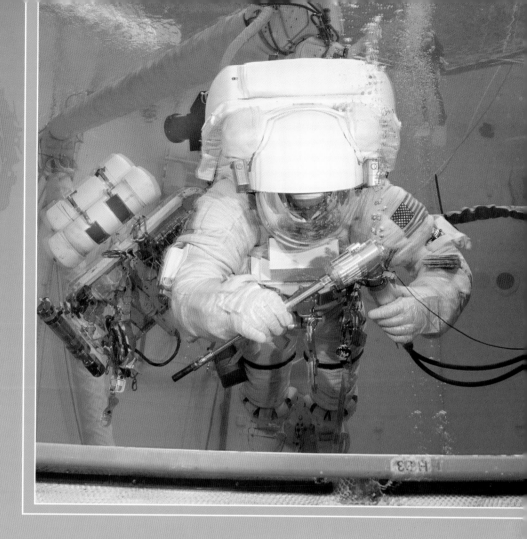

The Russian cosmonaut Yuri Gagarin, the first man to journey into space, blasted off from Earth on April 12, 1961.

◀ TOUGH TRAINING

Apart from learning how to operate a space vehicle, astronauts also have to prepare themselves for conditions in space. The biggest difference they encounter is weightlessness. In space, everything floats about—including the astronauts inside the spacecraft. Astronauts train for this in a specially designed swimming pool where they wear a modified spacesuit that allows them to float in the water without sinking or rising to the surface. This is called "neutral buoyancy," and astronauts reckon it's pretty close to being in space.

OUT OF THIS WORLD

Being selected to go into space is difficult, but there is a new way of getting there—space tourism. The Russian space program will take paying customers in a bid to raise funds to keep the program running. The only problem is that it is very expensive; a vacation that is literally out of this world will cost you $20 million.

◀ COOL WHEELS

When the American Apollo missions landed on the Moon during the 1960s and 1970s, a new form of transport was devised—the lunar rover. It was a battery-powered vehicle specially designed for use on the Moon. As the Moon's gravity is around one-sixth of the Earth's, the wheels were made from a kind of wire mesh. On Earth, these wheels aren't strong enough to hold the weight of two passengers, but on the Moon they are perfect. The three rovers that were used on the Moon are still up there to this day.

COSMIC DANGERS

S pace is an inhospitable place to be and without the proper equipment a human wouldn't last very long. However, even with the best planning and technology there are still many dangers.

▼ RAINING STONES

You don't have to travel into space to get injured by it. Meteors are lumps of rock that get pulled toward Earth by the planet's gravity. Most meteors burn up in the atmosphere and these streaks of light are often called "shooting stars." Sometimes, however, meteors survive all the way down to the ground and are known as meteorites. These can have disastrous results, though you'd be very unlucky to be hit by one.

▲ DEADLY DARK

Black holes are one of the most mysterious and dangerous objects in space. Black holes are possibly the remains of massive dead stars; they are so dense that their gravitational pull drags everything in toward them like a whirlpool. Even light itself can't escape. Unfortunately, this also means we can't see what's going on.

WASTE DISPOSAL ▶

It's not just natural hazards falling to Earth that you need to worry about. The night sky is full of man-made trash, such as old satellites or bits of rockets or even stuff that astronauts have dropped. This often finds its way back home, though it usually lands in the sea rather than in someone's backyard.

TRAGEDY ▶

Spacecraft are very complicated and expensive pieces of machinery, and a lot of time and trouble is taken to make sure they are working properly. Unfortunately, things don't always go according to plan and occasionally there are tragic results. Throughout the history of space travel, astronauts have died when their vehicles malfunctioned. Even the space shuttle has had faults and both the *Challenger* and *Columbia* were destroyed during their missions, killing everyone on board.

Our thirst for knowledge has seen us send hundreds of spacecraft into orbit in little over fifty years. Man-made objects orbit the Earth at around 22,000 miles per hour.

USEFUL SPACE

S pace may seem like a long way away, but people have been using it ever since ancient times. Whether it's for finding our way around or conducting complex experiments, we all have to be grateful to the sky above us.

▼ GETTING AROUND

Our ancient ancestors studied the stars and noticed that they seemed to be grouped into patterns. They called these groups "constellations," and they also recognized that some stars were brighter than others. These bright stars are called navigational stars as they helped sailors to find their way in the open oceans when they were far from land. Even today, these fifty-seven stars can still be used when getting about on the water.

▲ BIG INFLUENCE

As the Moon is so close to us—in space terms—it is not surprising to learn that it has a huge influence on the Earth. The most noticeable effect is that it pulls the world's oceans toward it as it orbits Earth—which is why we get high tides and low tides. And, without tides, life on Earth would suffer dramatically.

▶ EXPERIMENTAL

Space provides a unique environment, which science has been quick to capitalize on. One of the main roles of the International Space Station is for scientific study. Not only does it give scientists an unparalleled view of Earth from which to study weather patterns, it also provides a clear look at the universe. Also, the lack of gravity on board allows experiments to be carried out that would be impossible on Earth, as materials such as crystals grow and act differently back home.

Orion is the only constellation that can be seen from both the Northern and Southern Hemispheres of Earth.

NEXT STEP

So far, the only place humans have set foot other than our own planet is the Moon, and no one has been there since the 1970s. However, NASA has plans to build a base on the Moon and it hopes to have it done by 2020. The base could be used to explore the Moon itself and as a launch point for future missions, possibly to Mars.

FUTURE SPACE

Our achievements in space travel, great though they are, are still only the tip of the iceberg. There's so much left to do and explore and there are some really exciting plans in the pipeline.

BIG SLEEP

The biggest problem facing humans trying to explore space is the great distances involved. The nearest large galaxy to us is over two million light-years away, so even if we could build a spaceship that could travel really fast, the human pilots would be dead long before they arrived. The answer seems to be suspended animation—basically slowing down the human body so it doesn't age. It may seem a far-fetched idea, but scientists have already managed to do it for a short period with mice!

CIVILIAN SPACEMAN ▼

In 2001, the American Dennis Tito made history when he became the world's first space tourist. He spent nearly eight days in orbit as a crew member on a Russian rocket, paying a visit to the International Space Station. Since then, several other private space explorers from a number of different countries have made the trip, including the first female space tourist, who spent eight days on the ISS in 2006.

DENNIS A. TITO
ДЕННИС А. ТИТО

▲ BACK TO THE MOON

In 1969, Neil Armstrong became the first person to step onto the Moon. Since then, a grand total of only twelve people have visited our nearest neighbor, but things may be about to change; there are plans to build a base on the Moon. The base would work as a laboratory and as a launch pad for other space missions. As the gravity on the Moon is six times weaker than Earth's, it would take a lot less fuel to reach escape velocity, making space exploration much cheaper.

A light-year is the distance something would travel if it moved at the speed of light for a year.

OFF TO MARS? ▶

During the 1960s there was a "space race" between America and Russia and the winner was the first one to get to the Moon. Now a new space race is beginning and the objective is to get a person to Mars. Before that can happen, though, a number of probes need to land on the planet to tell us what the conditions there are really like. After all, it would be a shame to travel all that way only for an astronaut to get frazzled the minute he steps out of his rocket!

JUNGLE

RAINFORESTS

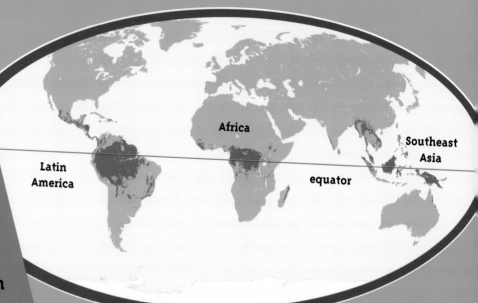

Latin America
Africa
equator
Southeast Asia

W hen people say jungle, they usually mean tropical rainforest. Rainforests are found around the equator—the imaginary line that circles the middle of the Earth. There are rainforests in Africa, Central and Southern America, Asia, and Australia.

◄ SAME BUT DIFFERENT

There are different types of tropical rainforest. The majority of the rainforest is called lowland forest, where it is warm all year round and it rains practically every day. On higher land, forests are often surrounded by clouds, hence their name of cloud forests. There are also monsoon or moist forests. Farther away from the equator there are monsoon or moist forests, where the rain does not fall in an even pattern throughout the year.

WET, WET, WET

The name is a giveaway really, but if you don't like getting wet, the rainforest is not the place for you. The weather in the lowland rainforests is very humid. There's always moisture in the air—either falling from the sky or rising as evaporation. These are ideal conditions for many plants to grow in—and they grow quickly. Each plant fights for its slice of sunlight, rising higher and higher toward the sky. As a result the forest floor is a pretty dark place to be.

CROWDED HOUSE

Rainforests cover only about 6 percent of the Earth's surface, but it's believed they are home to around 50 percent of the world's plants and animals. In just 2½ acres of land it's possible to spot hundreds of different species of tree, and thousands of birds, animals, and insects.

◄ FROM THE GROUND UP

The rainforest is generally split into four levels, each with its own species of plants and animals. Starting at the bottom there is, pretty obviously, the forest floor—the largest of the forest animals are found here. Next is the understory, which is the term for the smaller plants and young trees. Continue upward and you come to the canopy, which means among the branches to you and me. Finally you get to the emergents—they're the show-offs of the tree world, which grow taller than everyone else. They get more sunlight than the other trees, but are usually the first to fall down in high winds, too. Serves them right!

As jungles are such difficult places to explore, we know that many of the plants and animals there are yet to be discovered. New species are being discovered all the time—who knows how many new varieties are out there.

ANIMAL LIFE

Although the Central American rainforest is one of the smaller tropical forests, the South American Amazon rainforest is the world's largest. Together they have the biggest range of animals found anywhere on Earth.

Sloths spend so much of their time resting that even plants have time to grow on them— they are covered in green algae!

▼ EAGLE-EYED PREDATOR

You may think that being able to climb to the tops of the trees would keep you safe from predators, but that's not the case here. The fearsome harpy eagle—one of the world's largest eagles—swoops over the treetops of Central and South America. It's powerful enough to hunt animals as large as monkeys.

◀ THE BEAR FACTS

The popular children's book character of Paddington Bear was based on South America's spectacled bear. As you might imagine, these shy creatures don't share Paddington's fondness for marmalade sandwiches. In reality, South America's only type of bear eats fruit, nuts, plants, and some small animals.

A RIVER RUNS THROUGH IT

The Amazon rainforest gets its name from the mighty Amazon River, which flows for around 4,000 miles from the Andes Mountains down through the jungle to the Atlantic Ocean. It may not be the world's longest (it gets beaten by the Nile) but it carries more water than any other river. It's also home to thousands of species of animals including river dolphins, turtles, anacondas, and the ferocious piranha fish.

▶ TOXIC

Of course, you don't have to be big to be dangerous, and with the poison dart frog the clue to their deadly nature is in the name. The frog can make poison ooze from its skin and it's deadly enough to kill a monkey-sized animal. South American tribespeople use the poison to tip their blowpipe darts for hunting. There are over seventy species of poison dart frog, though a few of them aren't actually poisonous. The general rule is if they're colorful, they're toxic, so watch out!

AFRICAN JUNGLE

Most of the African rainforest is found in the area known as Central Africa. It is the second largest area of rainforest after the Amazon, and spreads over a number of different countries.

▲ JUNGLE ARMY

Even large animals have reason to fear one of the smallest predators in the jungle. Driver ants move in great armies consisting of millions of individuals. They have a ferocious bite, and there have been reports of driver ants eating goats, cows, and even elephants!

◄ GENTLE GIANT

One animal that has suffered from a poor reputation in the past is the gorilla. Often thought to be violent creatures, these close relatives of humans are actually quite gentle and intelligent. They live in groups called troops led by the dominant male known as a silverback due to—yes, you guessed it—the gray hairs on his back.

WHO'S A PRETTY BOY THEN? ▶

Although not as vibrantly colorful as some of the macaws found in rainforests around the world, the gray parrot is one of the most talkative parrots. Unfortunately, its ability to mimic sounds has also led to it becoming one of the forest's many endangered animals. Trade in these intelligent birds has been illegal for many years, but poaching still goes on.

Believe it or not, gorillas sleep in nests, either on the ground or in trees. They're quite loose constructions—but they do build a new one every night.

▼ FRUITFUL

Like all rainforests, the African jungle is home to thousands of fruits and edible plants. Coffee, yams, bananas, plantains, and palm oil are just a few of the foodstuffs that are valuable to people living in Africa.

LITTLE AND LARGE

You'd think that spotting an animal as big as an elephant wouldn't be so tricky—never mind a whole herd of them—but the African rainforest is so dense that it has made studying forest elephants very problematic. It's only fairly recently that scientists realized they were actually a completely different species to their larger elephant cousins, which live on the African savannah.

ASIAN JUNGLE

The rainforests of Asia cover a wide area stretching from the Indian subcontinent to Indonesia and down through New Guinea. This wide-ranging area is home to a huge variety of plants and animals.

▼ OLD MAN

If you're in Indonesia and you're really lucky you might spot an old man—but we're not talking about retirees here. The orangutan is often referred to as the old man of the forest. This retiring and intelligent ape is one of mankind's closest relatives, but it rarely comes down to the ground so it's difficult to see. Instead, it's happiest swinging through the trees with its long, powerful arms.

STINKER ▶

The jungles of Borneo are home to the world's largest flower. It's called the rafflesia and its flower can grow up to three feet across. But before you head off to the garden center to try to buy one, there is a major problem with this particular plant. Its size is matched by its smell—basically, it stinks of rotting meat. Not the sort of thing you want in your yard really!

▼ PASSENGERS

Plants like rafflesia are parasites—they feed off other plants. But in the Asian jungles there is another type of plant that grows on trees but isn't parasitic. They're called epiphytes and, like this bird's nest fern, they just use the trees to hitch a ride up to where the light is better.

▲ SPOT THE PREDATOR

Many jungle animals use camouflage to hide in the shadows—this is as true of insects as it is of big predators such as leopards and tigers. The cloud leopard's bold markings may stand out in a safari park, but in its natural home those spots match the dappled light and shade of the jungle perfectly.

Asian rainforests are home to the reticulated python—the longest species of snake in the world. They can grow to over 30 feet long!

AUSTRALIA

Although the Australian rainforest is small compared with others found across the world, it doesn't mean that it's not spectacular. Australia's remoteness from other large landmasses has allowed its wildlife to evolve in unique and surprising ways.

▲ NIGHT CRAWLER

One creature found only in the Australian rainforest is the green ringtail possum which, like the tree kangaroo, spends the majority of its time aboveground. Like many rainforest animals, it is nocturnal, which means it is active at night. The advantage of a nocturnal lifestyle is that there are fewer predators about when it is dark. During the day, the possum sleeps on a branch curled up in a tight ball.

◄ HOPPING ALONG

The last place you'd expect to see a kangaroo is in a tree, but that's exactly where you can spot them in this rainforest. There are eleven species of tree kangaroo in the world and some are so well adapted to their life in the branches they can barely hop on the ground anymore.

◀ FEELING BLUE

Rainforests are home to numerous insects, and some of the most colorful are the butterflies. One of the stars of the Australian jungle is the Ulysses butterfly, or the mountain blue as it is known. Being such a vivid blue color—and measuring nearly six inches across—it's one of the easier animals to spot in the rainforest.

Tree kangaroos and possums are both marsupials, which means they carry their young in pouches on their bellies. Australia has the biggest range of marsupials.

BEWARE OF THE PLANT

Of course, it's not just animals that can be a danger in the rainforest—sometimes the plants can cause pain and injury, too! The aptly named stinging tree produces leaves and stems covered in short hairs which, if touched, can stick into a person's body. What's more, the hairs are poisonous too, so on top of the cut you get an irritation that can last for months!

JUNGLE PEOPLE

The rainforests are not just home to a dazzling array of plants and animals. About fifty million people around the world call the jungle their home. Grouped into roughly 1,000 different tribes, these peoples have learned how to adapt to live in such a difficult environment.

▲ ON THE MOVE

Can you imagine having no permanent place to call home? Many rainforest people, like this member of the Huli tribe from Papua New Guinea, are hunter-gatherers. They get their food by hunting for animals or collecting edible plants. These tribes move around a lot as they have to live where food can be found.

► EXTREME FARMING

When tribes like the Yanomamo of Brazil do a bit of weeding, they don't use shears or hoes. Instead, they employ the slash-and-burn method—chopping down trees and burning the understory. The cleared ground is then planted with fruits and edible plants. After a year or two these fields are abandoned to be reseeded by the jungle.

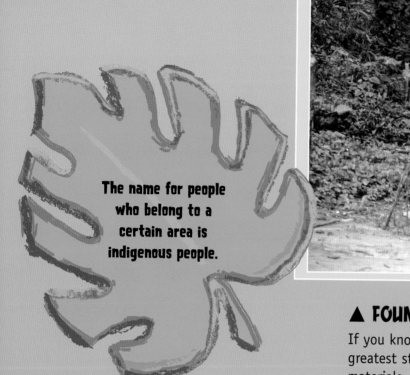

The name for people who belong to a certain area is indigenous people.

▲ FOUND IN THE FOREST

If you know what to look for, the rainforest is like the greatest store in the world! It provides food, building materials, clothes, and tools—and it's all free! This house, being built by a Mbuti woman from Zaire, is made from branches and leaves—a simple structure ideally suited to the Mbuti tribe's nomadic lifestyle.

DEADLY MEETING

For many tribes, their first meeting with people from Europe was a deadly one. The European explorers brought with them diseases like measles and smallpox—illnesses the rainforest people had never encountered before and had no natural resistance to. Tragically, whole tribes were wiped out through contact with Europeans.

▼ PROTESTING

The rights of the forest peoples have often been ignored. Industry and logging have taken over large areas of the forests they called home. Now some Amazon rainforest tribes are fighting back. Their high-profile protests, which have gained the support of pop stars like Sting, have secured the future of part of the forests for these tribes.

HOTTING UP

The world's jungles are shrinking at a phenomenal rate, and it's all down to the actions of humans. There is a real chance that the rainforests will be totally wiped out within fifty years—and then we'll be in deep trouble! Here's why . . .

▼ USEFUL PLANTS

Believe it or not, many of the drugs we use today originated from plants found in the rainforest. Although indigenous people have used healing plants for years, scientists are only really discovering them now. But with the rainforests fast disappearing, so are our chances of finding more useful medicines.

▲ CARBON COPY

Plants contain a lot of carbon and when trees are felled they release this carbon into the atmosphere as carbon dioxide—a major contributor to the greenhouse effect, which is causing our planet to warm up. The rainforests also absorb a significant amount of carbon dioxide, so the more trees that come down, the hotter things will be.

WASHED AWAY

Surprisingly, although rainforest trees grow very tall, the soil in the rainforest is only a few inches deep. This means that when the trees are gone it is very easy for all the soil to get washed away when it rains. This in turn leads to more forest clearance to make more fields—which will then get washed away. And so it goes on.

▼ FOOD FOR THOUGHT

Fancy a monkey burger? Or a slice of roast gorilla, perhaps? Although this might sound strange, in some places in Africa, bush meat—the name given to dead jungle animals—has become a staple part of people's diets. Often this is illegal and is pushing some species of animal close to extinction.

Some environmentalists estimate that an area of rainforest the size of a football field is cleared every second!

▼ TIMBER!

The most obvious threat to the rainforests comes from logging. Huge areas of rainforest—some larger than some countries—have been cut down to create farmland and to supply the timber industry. The cleared land is used to plant soya beans or coffee, or is used as grazing land. The irony is that the rainforest soil is not actually very fertile, so all the nourishment is used up very quickly and then more land has to be cleared.

OCEANS

WORLD OF WATER

O ver 70 percent of our planet's surface is covered in water and the majority of it is seawater. Most of this water can be divided into five large areas called oceans even though, in reality, all of the oceans are joined together.

The oceans account for around 97 percent of all the Earth's water.

▲ IN THE MIDDLE

The Indian Ocean is the body of water between Australia and the east coast of Africa. It is the third largest ocean and holds about a fifth of all the oceans' water.

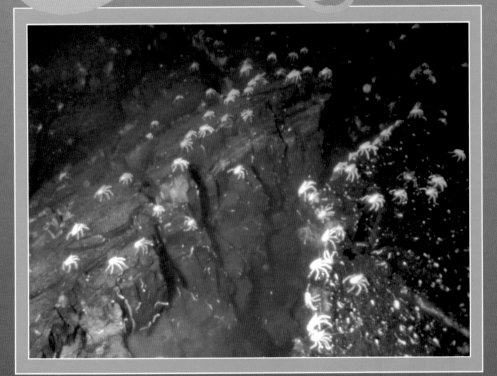

◄ THE BIGGEST

The largest ocean in the world is the Pacific, which is almost as big as all the other oceans put together. The Pacific is also the world's deepest ocean and is home to many huge undersea mountains and deep trenches. The deepest part of the Pacific is called the Challenger Deep in the Mariana Trench, which is an amazing seven miles below the surface of the waves!

► BUSY SEA

The second largest ocean is also one of the busiest. As the Atlantic Ocean separates the United States from Europe, a lot of sea traffic crosses the water between these continents.

A NEW ONE

In 2000, scientists named a new ocean, the Southern Ocean. It had always been there, of course, but in the past it had been included as part of the other oceans. Scientists realized that the area of water around Antarctica had its own unique traits, so it was agreed that it should form its own, distinct ocean. It is now the fourth largest of the oceans.

▼ THE SMALLEST

The smallest of the world's oceans is the Arctic, which is the area of water around the North Pole. Much of the Arctic Ocean is covered in ice, either packed together around the pole or floating about as icebergs.

WATERY HOME

The oceans are teeming with life from the microscopic to the massive. As with life on land, most sea life relies on sunlight to survive, so most living things in the ocean live in the zone where sunlight can penetrate the surface.

▼ ALL SORTS

Not all the animals that depend on the sea to survive actually live in the water full-time. Mammals like seals and sea lions and reptiles like marine iguanas stay on land to sleep and breed, only going to the oceans to hunt for food. Then there are seabirds— hundreds of different species that also rely on the oceans to survive. Most seabirds, like puffins, seagulls, and pelicans, either dive into the water to catch fish or skim across the surface for them. Penguins are expert swimmers, having lost the ability to fly but having gained flipper-like wings instead.

▲ SMALL BUT IMPORTANT

Plankton is the general name for the tiny creatures and plants that drift about in the sunlit zone of the ocean. There are billions of them— which is just as well as they are at the bottom of the food chain.

Most people think seaweed is a plant, but scientists call it algae. True plants have roots, leaves, seeds, or flowers—seaweed doesn't.

▶ NOT JUST FISH

The upper layers of the ocean are home to a staggering range of animal life. Obviously there are fish—thousands of different species from huge whale sharks to colorful tropical fish—but there are also jellyfish, snails, corals, anemones, and mammals such as dolphins, whales, and the rare manatee. Then there are reptiles too, such as sea snakes and seven different types of turtle.

◀ WEEDY WONDERS

The sunlit zone is the only part of the ocean that supports plant life and seaweed. One type of seaweed is called kelp and it can grow in large groups, called forests. Kelp forests are home to many types of sea creature, including seahorses. The dense seaweed provides plenty of places for these smaller creatures to hide and escape from predators.

INTO THE DEEP

The bottom of the ocean, where sunlight cannot penetrate, is a very different world from the teeming waters above. Here it is dark and cold. There is little oxygen in the water for animals to breathe and the pressure from the weight of the water above is enormous. Yet this forbidding place is home to a surprising array of ocean life.

▼ DEEP DIVING

Some creatures, such as the sperm whale, are only visitors to the dark zones of the oceans. Scientists do not know exactly how deep a sperm whale can dive but some think that it could be over 1¼ miles. One of the sperm whale's favorite foods is the giant squid, but how the whales can find them—or any other food—in the dark water is something of a mystery.

Sunken ships take a long time to rust in the deepest parts of the ocean because there is so little oxygen.

◄ IN HOT WATER

Not everywhere at the bottom of the ocean is cold. When cracks appear in the Earth's crust, cold water comes into contact with magma—molten rock that can be as hot as 2,000°F. The hot water is forced away from the crack, creating a watery volcano. This is called a deep sea vent and many species of fish, shrimp, crab, and octopus have adapted to live in these super-warm conditions.

YOU CAN'T SEE ME!

The vampire squid lives in waters up to 3,000 feet deep. Its jelly-like body is covered with light-producing organs, which it can turn off when it wants to, making itself completely invisible to both its prey and its predators.

► BRIGHT LIGHT

Many deep-sea fish are equipped to generate their own light. Female anglerfish have what looks like a rod sticking out above their mouths. At the end of the rod is a piece of flesh that glows. This attracts not only small fish, which the anglerfish quickly snaps up in its toothy jaws, but also male anglerfish with which to mate.

71

WORK AND PLAY

People have made their living from the oceans for thousands of years. However, the world's seas can be unpredictable places to work, so a job on the oceans always carries a risk of injury—or even death.

▲ ISOLATION

One of the most isolated places a person can work is on an oil platform in the middle of the ocean, drilling for oil on the seabed. As these platforms are often many miles from shore, the workers stay there for two weeks at a time. The platforms have to be self-sufficient too, in case bad weather means that help cannot come in the event of an emergency. Each platform has its own doctor and even a mini hospital.

◄ TRAWLING THE OCEANS

One of the oldest jobs associated with the sea is that of fishing. Today, fishing boats catch over 198 million pounds of fish each year. The fish are caught by boats called trawlers, though these boats can be very different in size and in the way they are used. Many are equipped with onboard freezing equipment, which means the boats can stay at sea for weeks at a time. Sometimes large factory ships are used. These boats process the catch from many different trawlers and have huge freezer compartments for storing the fish.

▶ FUN ON THE WAVES

Not all human activity on the waves is hard work, of course. Water sports are always popular, like surfing, sailing, or just going for a swim. Offshore powerboating is one of the world's most expensive and fastest sports. These high-performance vessels can reach speeds in excess of 100 miles per hour—a phenomenal speed over water.

Nuclear submarines never run out of fuel. The only reason they need to come to the surface is for more provisions.

▼ BIG SHIPS

There are two different types of navy: the merchant navy, which consists of civilian ships carrying trade goods, and the military navy, which is part of a country's armed forces. The biggest armed ships are aircraft carriers, which can be over 1,000 feet long and carry a crew of more than 5,500 sailors.

EXPLORATION

As water covers so much of the planet, it was only a matter of time before humans felt the need to explore it. We are still exploring the oceans to this day and have yet to uncover all of their secrets.

The wreck of the Titanic will be completely destroyed in the next fifty years if it remains a tourist attraction.

▼ FLAT EARTH

It is thought people used to believe that the world was flat because of the straight edge seen on the horizon across the oceans. However, sailors knew this wasn't the case. They had always known that there was a curve to the Earth, as they had seen the way a boat could disappear over the horizon and then return safe and sound.

▲ TRADERS AND EXPLORERS

Historically, the first explorers of the oceans were seafaring traders and fishermen. Ancient civilizations such as the Phoenicians were always pushing back the boundaries of the known world as they traveled farther and farther to find new places to sell their wares. Many people believe that Basque fishermen from Spain and France were the first to cross the Atlantic to America as they searched for fish.

▶ LOOKING UNDERWATER

Exploring what lies beneath the waves has always been fascinating to people. Of course the biggest problem with underwater exploration is breathing underwater. As early as the fourth century BC the ancient Greeks had developed a kind of diving bell. This was an upturned container big enough for divers to stick their heads into to get a lungful of air before continuing with their work. The first diving helmet, complete with oxygen supply, was designed centuries later in 1829. It was based on the traditional knight-in-armor helmet.

▼ GOING DOWN

To explore the bottom of the sea, explorers and scientists use a machine called a bathyscaphe. These are like submarines, but are constructed to survive the water pressure at extreme depths. In 1960 a bathyscaphe called *Trieste* even made it to the bottom of the Mariana Trench, the deepest point on Earth.

WILD SEAS

As any sailor could tell you, the oceans can be hazardous places. A boat hundreds of miles from shore can fall victim to a variety of unpleasant forces of nature.

◄ FREAK WAVES

Every so often an especially large wave will surge across the oceans. No one is entirely sure why these rogue waves occur and hundreds of ships are believed to have been sunk by them. The waves can reach heights of over 100 feet and can affect even the biggest ships. In 1978 the cargo ship *München* was sunk by a freak wave and everyone on board was drowned.

◄ SPINNING AROUND

If you have ever watched how the water drains from a sink or bathtub then you've got a good idea of what a whirlpool looks like. Whirlpools can occur in the oceans and are generally the result of tidal activity. Although a whirlpool can be as much as 250 feet across, it is not strong enough to pull a boat into its swirling vortex. However, you would be crazy to swim near a whirlpool as it is more than capable of drowning a person.

One ship is lost every week on the world's oceans.

▲ OCEAN TWISTER

Tornadoes are deadly spirals of wind that can occur over land; waterspouts are their oceanic relatives. Waterspout winds can reach over 125 miles per hour and can cause terrible damage, mainly due to flying debris. What's more, if you see one waterspout you'll probably see another one, as they generally appear in groups.

◄ FLOATING MOUNTAINS

Icebergs are huge lumps of frozen fresh water that break off from glaciers and float free in the oceans. As the sinking of the *Titanic* proved, hitting an iceberg can have disastrous consequences. This is why there are now regular ice-spotting patrols in the Atlantic Ocean to warn ships of imminent problems.

OCEAN LEGENDS

T hroughout history, ships and boats have disappeared without a trace. There are good scientific explanations for these sudden disappearances, but in earlier unenlightened times strange stories circulated about what sailors could find in the oceans.

▼ FATAL SINGING

Mermaids were meant to be half-woman, half-fish. In some stories mermaids would lure sailors to their doom on jagged rocks with their beautiful voices. The most likely explanation was that sailors had spotted either seals or manatees in the water and had mistaken them for people. However, neither are particularly good singers.

▼ MISSING CITY

Plato, the ancient Greek writer, recorded the fate of Atlantis—an island in the Atlantic that disappeared into the sea. No one has ever found any proof that Atlantis existed but that has not stopped people speculating as to where it might have been. To ancient mariners wary of towering waves and violent storms, the idea of an island falling into the sea probably felt like an all-too-real possibility.

The peaks of undersea volcanoes can emerge gradually over a number of years to form small islands.

▲ TENTACLED TERROR

Tales of ships attacked by a huge octopus-like creature date back hundreds of years. It is quite possible that these stories may be based on sightings of a giant squid, an animal known to fight with sperm whales.

DAVY JONES' LOCKER

If you hear that someone has ended up in Davy Jones' locker, it means they have drowned at sea and their final resting place is a watery grave. The origin of the saying is not clear, but Davy Jones is thought to be an evil spirit of the deep.

SEA MONSTERS

TALL STORIES?

Legends of sea monsters have been told for as long as people have spent their evenings swapping stories. Seafarers have always come back with terrifying tales of mysterious creatures. There must be something about being at the mercy of the waves that messes with the mind—or is there something more to these unlikely myths?

▼ NERVOUS WRECK

What we have to remember is that sailing could be a terrifying experience. Battling stormy seas in leaky wooden boats was a constant reminder of how close a neighbor death could be. Explorers pushed the boundaries of the known world farther and farther, and with this came a natural fear of the unknown—and being lost and exhausted is bound to cause havoc with your nerves!

STRANGE WORLD ▶

Not all the blame for these tall tales lies with sailors, however. Regular seafarers were used to seeing creatures such as whales or sharks, but many of these sailors could not read or write. The passengers were often the literate ones, as they could afford education and travel. Imagine seeing a whale for the first time and not knowing what it was—you would probably think that you had seen a monster, too! Other scholars who wrote of sea monsters may not even have been to sea themselves at all, but were merely recounting tales that had been told to them.

▼ SCARE TACTICS

Sometimes, stories of sea monsters were not just used for entertainment. Some early traders deliberately spread rumors of sea monsters as a way of scaring off the competition from following their highly profitable trade routes. Why bother going all the way to a distant port when there was a good chance you'd end up as a light lunch for a creature from the deep?

Many old sea maps have pictures of monsters, partly as decoration, partly as warnings of the danger of the unknown.

MONSTER BONES

In the past, not everything had a simple explanation, so superstition replaced most things that today can be accounted for by science. Dinosaur bones on land helped fuel the belief in dragons—so why shouldn't monsters live in the sea, too? Such beliefs were supported when rotting carcasses of whales or other large marine creatures were washed ashore. The decayed corpses looked like nothing anyone had ever seen, and were rumored to be monsters.

ANCIENT TALES

L ife developed in the seas long before it did on land, so it'll come as no surprise that there have been some pretty scary creatures floating around our oceans in the past. The top predators on the planet used to live in the water—and here are some of the most impressive.

Sharks first appeared on Earth around 400 million years ago.

▼ SNAP, SNAP!

One type of ancient sea monster still with us today is the crocodile. The largest crocodile—the estuarine, or saltwater, crocodile—grows to more than 20 feet in length. This is impressive enough, but it's positively tiny compared to its ancient relatives. Some early forms of crocodile were absolutely huge—up to 40 feet long!

◄ TOOTHLESS TERROR

Over 360 million years ago, one fish not to be messed with was Dunkleosteus. At around 18 feet long, this armor-plated monster was bigger than today's great white shark. Although Dunkleosteus didn't have any teeth—each jaw had a hard bony edge instead—it was still the top predator of the day and was more than happy to eat anything that crossed its path.

MESOZOIC MAULER

One of the most fearsome creatures ever to roam the oceans was the Liopleurodon. It terrorized the seas during the Mesozoic era, around 150 million years ago. At around 50 feet in length, and with a ferocious reputation to match, it was more than big enough to be a worry to everything else in the ocean, and even attacked unwary dinosaurs paddling along the shore.

► INLAND SERPENTS

You may not even have to go to sea to spot monstrous serpents—some people believe that certain lakes are home to their own monsters. The most famous lake monsters are Nessie from Loch Ness in Scotland, Ogopogo from Lake Okanagan in British Columbia, Canada, and Champ from Lake Champlain in the United States. It has been claimed that these lakes may have underground passages to the ocean, allowing the monsters to meet other sea monsters and breed.

SEA SERPENTS

The classic sea monster is, of course, the sea serpent. There have been reports of gigantic snakelike terrors in the oceans for hundreds of years, but what's the real story behind this particular menace?

IN THE CAN

Chesapeake Bay, off the east coast of the United States, is reputedly home to a large sea serpent nicknamed Chessie. In 1982, a Chesapeake resident named Robert Frew spotted Chessie and managed to capture it—on videotape, that is. The tape was sent to the Smithsonian Institution to be examined but the quality was too poor for scientists to say exactly what Frew had seen. So is Chessie real, or an animal we already know—a seal or a manatee perhaps?

NESSIE ▼

Of course, one of the most famous monsters in the world is Nessie—rumored to inhabit Loch Ness in Scotland. Like many other lake monsters around the world, it is thought that Nessie is a living plesiosaur—a marine reptile dating from the time of the dinosaurs. Nessie-spotters often claim to have seen a long neck and a humpback, which is just what a plesiosaur looked like. Could this mean some ancient reptiles still exist?

In 1840, the crew of the Pekin were convinced they spotted a sea monster. It turned out to be a big clump of seaweed.

◀ FABULOUS FISH

One thing is beyond doubt—one kind of sea serpent does exist. Check out exhibit A, the oarfish. At around 30 feet long, and with a red dorsal fin running the length of its body, the oarfish looks quite unlike any other species of fish. Could this unusual beast be what sailors have been spotting for all these years?

▼ SNAKES ALIVE!

There are also snakes that swim in the sea. Some of these sea snakes have flattened bodies, which help them to swim and also make them look somewhat odd. Could reports of the river-dwelling anaconda of South America—which grows to over 30 feet in length—have helped convince people that monsters live in the ocean?

SUCKERED IN

T ake a peek at an octopus or a squid—it has looks only a mother could love. That rubbery texture and all those suckery legs writhing around like a nest of snakes is enough to give many people nightmares. Imagine how you would feel seeing a gigantic version of one of those bearing down on you if you were out for a swim.

There's plenty of evidence of giant squid—sperm whales are often found with huge sucker marks from fights with these massive creatures.

KRAKEN ▶

The most notorious of the ancient, squid-like monsters was the Kraken, and there have been many tales of these giant creatures rearing up out of the ocean and dragging boats down beneath the waves with them. It was claimed, in the 1700s—by the Bishop of Bergen, no less, so you'd hope he was telling the truth—that the Kraken was as big as an island. Now that would make a scary vacation destination!

MONSTERS IN PRINT

Seafarers have long told tales of giant octopus and squid attacking their ships. It's such a well-worn theme that these episodes have made it into books, too—most famously Jules Verne's *Twenty Thousand Leagues Under the Sea*. Of course, there's little reliable documentary evidence that such attacks ever occurred, but that doesn't mean such monsters don't exist.

GIANT OCTOPUS

Lusca is the name given to a type of giant octopus that is meant to live in the Caribbean. Legend has it that these monsters are around 130 feet long—around ten times bigger than the documented size for giant octopi. There's little proof that Luscas exist, of course, but a series of old photographs showing a mysterious body washed up in the Bahamas might suggest they are out there...

REAL-LIFE MONSTER ▶

Today, the closest thing we know of to the Kraken is the giant squid. Some scientists estimate that it could grow to around 40 feet in length—that's about the length of a bus. There is some evidence, however, of a colossal squid that could possibly be twice the size of the giant squid— that's a lot of calamari!

FISH FOOD!

The fear sailors had of sea monsters was twofold. First, the monster might sink the ship, leaving the sailors either to drown or be cast adrift to a slow death. Second, the monster might fancy a sailor-snack and eat them. But how likely is it that a person could get eaten at sea?

The throats and stomachs of most whales and sharks are too small to swallow a human.

▼ DEADLY TASTER

Of course, sailors may well have seen people eaten by some types of shark. Undoubtedly, sharks such as the great white and tiger shark have eaten and do eat people, but humans aren't their favorite food. Most attacks are actually the shark having a quick taster, only to leave the victim alone after realizing that it's not the type of snack they're after.

THE LEGEND OF JONAH ▶

The idea of being swallowed by a sea monster is ingrained in myths, legends, and even religion. The Bible tells a story of a man called Jonah who was swallowed by a large fish. After he prayed to God, the fish let him go.

◀ BIG FISH

Would it be possible to be eaten by a basking or whale shark? After all, they are the two biggest types of fish in the sea (remember, whales are mammals). However, these two sharks eat tiny sea creatures and aren't likely to swallow something as big as a man.

▶ TINY MEALS

Whales certainly look big enough to eat a person, and they are the biggest animals in the sea. However, many whales eat tiny sea creatures called krill, which they trap in comb-like plates of bone in their mouths called baleen. It's difficult to imagine that a baleen whale would want to—or could—eat a human. Other whales have teeth, and the biggest of these is the sperm whale. Interestingly, there is a tale that a sailor called James Bartley was swallowed alive by a sperm whale during the 1890s and survived for sixteen hours in the whale's stomach!

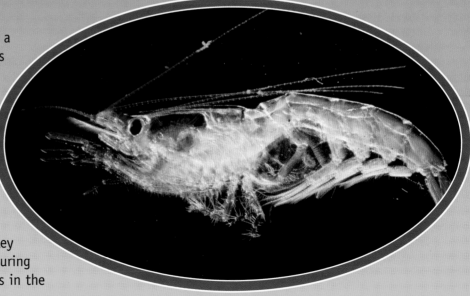

DEEP AND DARK

As we have seen, not all sea monsters are figments of people's imaginations. In truth, the oceans are home to some of the strangest animals you could imagine—and some of the oddest are found at the very bottom of the sea.

▼ TOOTHY MONSTER

Some of the scariest teeth to be found in the ocean belong to the viperfish—they're so big they can't even fit inside the fish's mouth. Fortunately, the fish is only ten inches long, so it's not a real threat to anything large.

▼ LURING THEM IN

The bottom of the ocean is so far from the surface that even sunlight can't get down all that way. Instead, sea creatures here produce their own light. The aptly named anglerfish uses a glowing ball of light hanging from its dorsal fin to attract small fish, like an angler with a baited hook. When the fish get close, the anglerfish suddenly springs to life and gulps the hapless victim down.

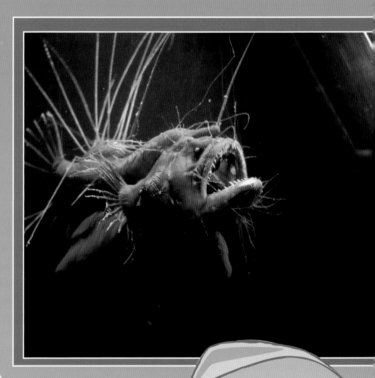

Some scientists believe that up to 90 percent of deep-sea fish can produce their own light.

GULP! ▶

The gulper eel has two big advantages for a deep-sea predator—a huge mouth and an expanding stomach. The gulper eel's already large mouth can actually unhinge, or dislocate, allowing it to swallow prey as big as itself. Fortunately, its stomach can stretch just as much to accommodate the eel's sizable lunch.

▼ JEEPERS CREEPERS

The Greenland shark's shining eyes make it look more menacing than it really is—actually it's quite a harmless creature. This rare shark is one of the few that live in Arctic waters, where it can be found in both deep and shallow water. One of the largest sharks, the light in its eyes is produced by a parasite that lives on the poor shark's peepers.

WHAT WAS THAT?

T he only way to tell for sure whether there are sea monsters in our oceans is to find them. Unfortunately, that's easier said than done. There's a lot of water out there—it covers more than 70 percent of the planet—and these sea creatures can be very elusive.

Cryptids is the name given by cryptozoologists to the mysterious monsters they search for that are so far unrecognized by science.

MEGA SURPRISE

We can be fairly sure that there are some big sea creatures that we don't know about, but finding them seems to be a matter of luck. Until 1976, no one knew that the megamouth shark even existed, and then one was caught by a research vessel. If something as big as this 16-foot shark can stay hidden for all this time, then perhaps there really are some big monsters out there.

BEACHCOMBING

Sometimes scientists don't have to go looking for interesting creatures. Instead, the sea washes them up, or fishermen net them by mistake. Generally, these creatures have been dead for a long time and are badly decomposed. In 1977, a Japanese trawler hauled what looked like a dead plesiosaur from the waves. There was great excitement—until scientists pointed out that this is exactly what basking sharks look like as they rot.

◄ SCIENTISTS OR NUTS?

The practice of looking for animals that most people consider to be either myths or extinct is called cryptozoology. Many people pour scorn on cryptozoologists, declaring them not to be proper scientists. However, some cryptozoologists do use very strict scientific criteria in their work.

▼ SECRET PLACES

Most of the sea remains unexplored, mainly because it's quite difficult to study such a large area properly. Also, the seabed isn't nice and flat. Instead it's made up of mountains and trenches—some more than seven miles deep—so there are plenty of places for creatures to hide.

HUMAN BODY

AMAZING US!

We live on an amazing planet full of extraordinary things, but your body is just as awesome in its own way. Look at all the things that make you what you are: skin, hair, blood, muscles, organs, veins—to name just some of the parts. And what's more, it all fits together in one neat package. Take a closer look at your body and you'll be really surprised what's going on in there.

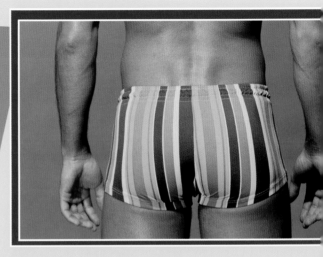

▲ BIG AND SMALL

Your body is a combination of large and small pieces. The largest muscle in your body is the gluteus maximus, but you might find it a bit difficult to see exactly how big it is because it's behind you—it's your rear. The smallest bone in your body is the stirrup bone, which is only $\frac{1}{10}$ inch long and is inside your ear.

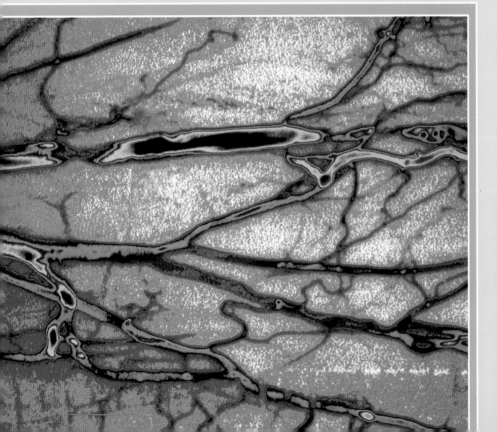

◄ TUBES

Your body is stuffed full of tubes, or veins as they are called, and this is how the blood travels around your body. If you could take all the veins out of a body and lay them end to end they would stretch for over 60,000 miles! That's far enough to wrap around the Moon nine times!

► STRETCHY

Apart from having all those miles of veins and hundreds of different bits and pieces, your body is also fantastically flexible. From birth, you will grow for around eighteen years and be about five times taller than you were when you were born. Even when you're fully grown you can still expand. Think about a pregnant woman and how her womb has to get bigger to accommodate that baby—her body needs to be really stretchy to allow the bump to stick out.

A cell is like a microscopic chemical package. Your body is made up of millions of cells—so many that scientists can't really say how many there are.

◄ OVERCOMING FLAWS

Although the way the body works is just one of nature's marvels, it's not perfect. For a start, we have quite large heads, which we need to fit our oh-so-intelligent brains into. Unfortunately all this weight at the top of our relatively long bodies makes us quite unstable—that's why toddlers fall down so often. However, as we've survived this long, there can't be too much wrong with us!

SUPER STRUCTURE

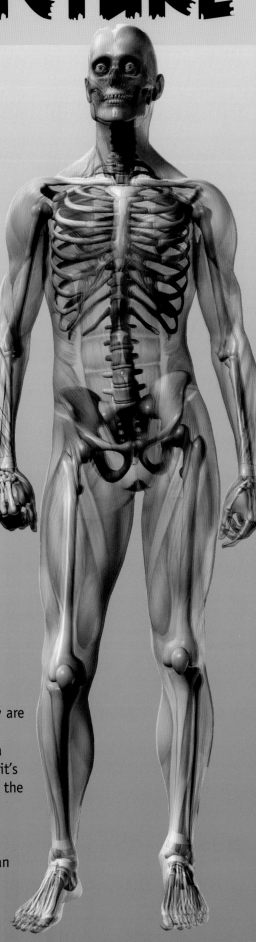

That wonderful body of yours would be nothing but a sack of blood and organs without your bones. It's our arrangement of bones that makes humans look like humans, but that's not the only job bones do—your skeleton is really a super structure.

▶ MISSING BONES?

You have a lot more bones than you probably realize; in fact you have a whopping 206 of them. But before you get too pleased with yourself, that's nothing compared to babies—they've got over 300 bones. So where do these extra bones go? Nowhere—babies' bones are quite soft and many of them fuse together before they harden, reducing the number to just over 200 as they grow older.

◀ HARD SPONGE

Your bones may hold you up, but they are not solid—if they were they'd be very heavy. The inside of our bones looks a little like a honeycomb or a sponge—it's filled with lots of tiny holes. This has the advantage of making your bones both strong and light. This honeycomb structure is surrounded by a smooth, hard outside, which is the part you can see when you look at the bone.

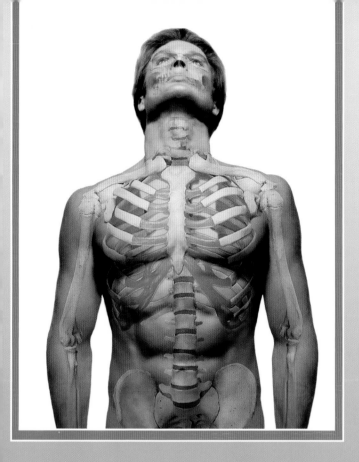

◀ MULTITASKING

Your bones don't just make you human-shaped—they perform other important roles, too. The way your bones are arranged to make your skeleton means they provide a useful protection service. For instance, your ribs protect your lungs and heart and your skull protects your brain. That's not all—inside your bones is a substance called marrow and this produces your blood cells. You'll find out more about what they do later on.

Some young bones are made from cartilage, which is the same stuff that a shark's skeleton is made from (and the part at the end of your nose).

◀ GROWING

Obviously, as you grow up your bones get bigger—otherwise you'd stay child-sized forever. In fact, your bones continue to get bigger until your late teens. But when you reach your twenties it doesn't mean that that's it. Your bones are always renewing themselves; old parts of bone dissolve and new parts replace them. It's just as well the new parts grow—you know what we'd look like without any bones!

ON THE INSIDE

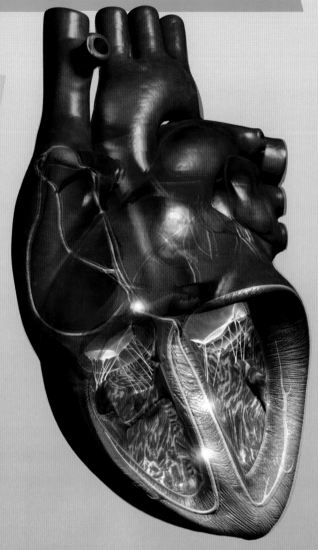

Everything inside your body is there for a reason, but some of the most important components are your organs. These are individual parts of the body that do a specific job. You've got lots of them in your body, but here are some of the major ones.

HEART OF THE MATTER ▶

The heart is a muscle that moves the blood around your body. The blood flows into the heart through the veins, passing through four different chambers inside it before exiting the heart through other veins. When you feel your heart beating, it is the muscle pumping the blood from one chamber to the next. It does this around seventy times a minute and never stops, day or night—if it does you're in big trouble!

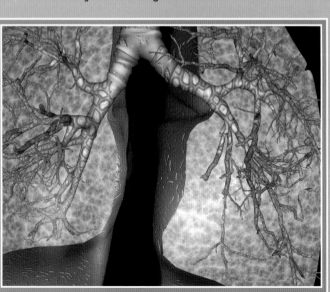

◀ DEEP BREATH

Every time you take a breath you can feel your lungs at work as they make your chest move as they fill with air. Your lungs aren't like big air-filled balloons though—it's more a case of a big bag with lots of little bags inside it. The lungs are filled with little veins and tiny air sacs, which in turn are surrounded by blood vessels. The vessels take the air from the sacs and move it around your body.

KIDNEYS ▶

Your kidneys are two fist-sized organs that are the waste-reprocessing plant of your body. They take all the things your body doesn't need from your blood and get rid of any extra water. The kidneys send this liquid waste to the bladder, where it's stored until you go to the bathroom. The kidneys also control the amount of various chemicals in your blood—too many would be bad news, so these little organs have a big job to do.

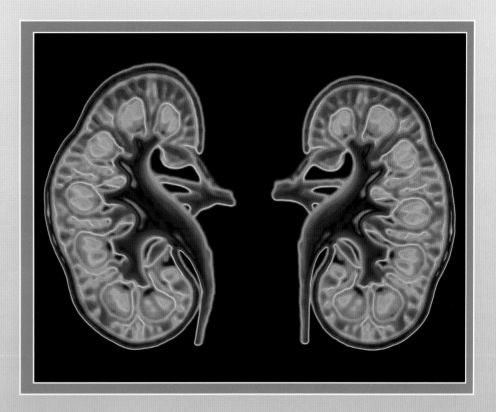

One organ you have but don't need anymore is your appendix. Some scientists think it helped our ancestors to digest tough food that humans no longer eat.

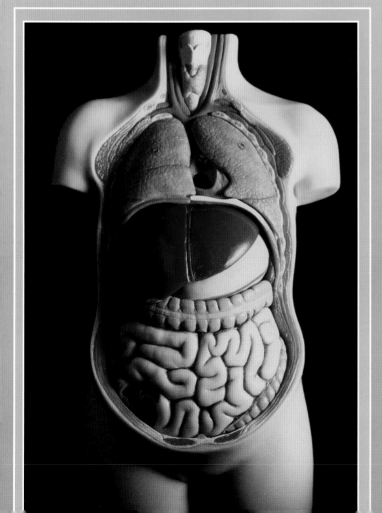

◀ HARDWORKING LIVER

The biggest organ inside your body is your liver. It works like a big factory, making chemicals that your body needs from the nutrients that you eat. It also helps to guard the body by producing the substance that allows the blood to clot—which is useful, because without this we'd bleed to death if we got cut. The liver also produces bile, which helps the body to digest the food you eat. With so many jobs, it's not surprising the liver is so big.

ON THE OUTSIDE

All those bones, blood vessels, tubes, and organs would be just one big mess on the floor if it wasn't for your skin to keep it all in. But don't think for one minute your skin is just a big bag—it's much more interesting than that.

STRETCHY ORGAN ▶

Your skin is actually your body's biggest organ and does some really important jobs. It acts like a living suit of armor, keeping out germs and harmful ultraviolet rays from the Sun. It also acts as a layer of insulation, keeping the body at a reasonable temperature as well as keeping water out.

◀ STRAIGHT OR CURLY?

The holes in our skin that hair comes out of are called follicles. You've got lots of them—over a million in fact—and the shape of your follicles decides what kind of hair you have. A curly shaped follicle results in curly hair and a straight follicle means straight hair.

BUMPS ▶

The hair that grows out of your skin adds another level of insulation, but we have a lot less hair than our ancestors did—mainly because we don't need it anymore. It's also the reason we get goosebumps. When our bodies get cold the skin contracts and this pushes the hair up off the skin. In furry animals this would increase the amount of air trapped between the hairs, which would help to keep them warm. On our not-so-hairy bodies all it does is give us bumpy skin.

Your skin is dying and regrowing all of the time—a lot of the dust you see around you is actually dead skin!

LAYER UPON LAYER ▶

Your skin is made of three separate layers and they all do different things. The outside layer is called the epidermis and keeps everything outside the body from getting inside. The middle layer, or the dermis as it is called, is where your hair grows from. It also has all your sweat glands—sweating is your body's way of cooling down. The bottom layer, or hypodermis, is there to keep your skin attached to the rest of your body. Without the hypodermis your skin would hang off your bones like an old sack—not a good look!

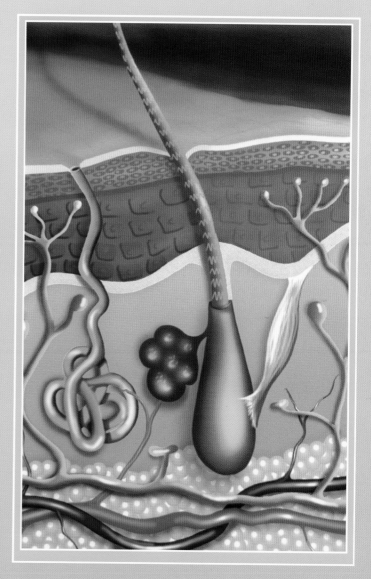

VITAL SENSES

Your senses provide you with awareness of your environment. Without them you wouldn't know what was around you—which would be a problem if you were being stalked by a tiger, for example. So your senses really do make sense.

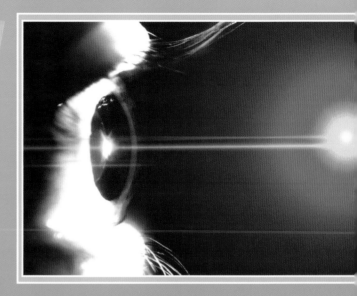

▲ LOOK OUT

There's a lot going on when you look at something. The light coming from the image of what you are looking at enters the eye, where it's flipped upside down and is projected onto something called the retina at the back of your eye. This signal travels to your brain along the optic nerve, where the brain flips the image the right way up. Your eyes also tell you how far away an object is and what color it is. Staring at one thing for too long can strain the eyes, which is one reason why you should not watch too much TV—those eyes need protecting!

▼ TOUCHY FEELY

Your body is covered in thousands of nerve endings found in the bottom layer of your skin. These send messages to the brain whenever your skin touches something. Most of your touch receptors are grouped in specific parts of your body, such as your fingertips and your tongue. This is useful—imagine if you had to rub your nose on everything to find out what it felt like!

STINKY ▶

Your ability to taste things wouldn't be anywhere near as good if you couldn't smell them too. Your nose is much more discerning than your tongue and can pick out hundreds of different smells. In fact, your senses of taste and smell are so closely linked that food doesn't taste the same if you've got a stuffy nose. Smells are also very good at triggering memories, but we're not entirely sure why this is useful.

Generally people think that there are only five senses—but there are more. Most scientists would add the ability to feel heat, cold, pain, and balance to the list.

◀ TASTY!

Your ability to taste things rests—literally—on your tongue, which is covered in tiny taste receptors. When you think of all the different flavors of things you like to eat you'd think that these receptors must be pretty complex, but in fact they can only distinguish between five different tastes—bitter, sweet, sour, salt, and umami. This last one sounds a bit odd, but it is a specific taste that comes with many foods including meat and cheese. So if you like cheeseburgers, these taste receptors will be working pretty hard.

BRAIN BOX

You can remove pretty much everything from your body—including your heart—and replace it for a while with a machine and keep on living. But take out your brain and there's nothing that can replace it. That's because your brain keeps the whole show on the road.

TAXI!

Different thoughts or actions are dealt with by different parts of your brain. The right-hand side is responsible for your creativity, while the left-hand side is in charge of the more logical and scientific stuff. What's more, if you use one area of your brain a lot, it gets bigger. Famously, New York cab drivers have to remember lots of streets and routes, and as a result the bit of their brain they use to remember such things is bigger than average.

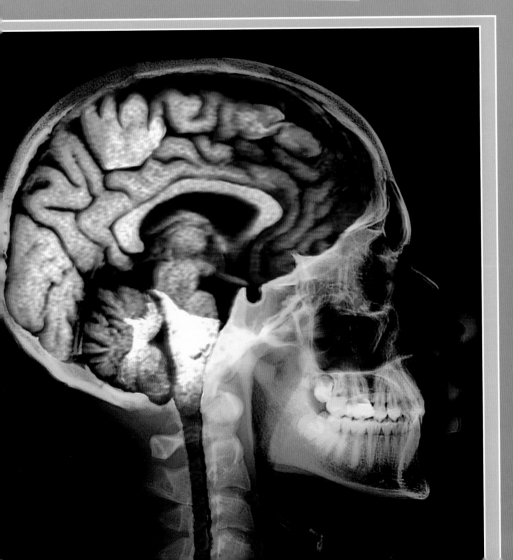

◀ WHAT IT DOES

Your brain is really your body's very own supercomputer. It processes all the information that your senses send it, from what you're touching to the upside-down images on your retina. Your brain does all your thinking, and governs your movements, controls your breathing, and stores your memories. Like your heart, it works 24/7—when you're asleep your brain doesn't knock off for the night too. In fact, when you dream, your brain is just as active as it is during the day.

GLOWING ▶

Scientists don't know exactly how the brain works, but they can monitor its activity using special scanners. The scanners show scientists and doctors which parts of the brain are active by lighting up the areas being used. This helps our understanding of how the brain works—as well as providing some very pretty pictures!

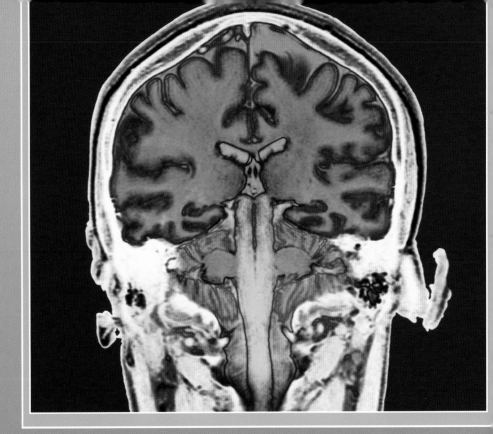

The more you use your brain, the better it works—but don't think too much, as it really can tire your brain out!

◀ WHAT IT LOOKS LIKE

For such a vital bit of your body, your brain doesn't look like much—it's a bit like a squidgy peach stone. There are three separate parts to your brain. The cerebrum is the largest part and is split into two halves called hemispheres. Below that is a part called the cerebellum, and coming out from the bottom is the brain stem. As the brain is so important, it is protected by the skull, and to keep the brain from banging against the skull it is surrounded by thin membranes and fluid. Even then, a bad blow on the head can damage your brain—you wouldn't drop a computer on the floor, so you have to be careful with your brain, too.

UNDER ATTACK

Like any other fantastic machine, your body has to be well looked after. What makes things difficult is that your body is under constant attack—and a lot of the time you can't even see what's attacking you.

▼ KEEP OUT!

Your body has a number of ways of tackling diseases. Obviously the best thing to do is to stop them from getting into your body in the first place. That first layer of defense is one of the main jobs of your skin, but that's not your only natural barrier. Inside your nose and throat you have special tissues that produce mucus—or what you might call snot. The mucus traps bacteria that you breathe in. So next time you complain about a stuffy nose, just remember that most of the time that snot is doing you good!

WIGGLY WORMS ▲

The world is crammed full of bacteria, but you wouldn't know as they are microscopically small. Bacteria are everywhere, even inside our bodies. Some of them are good and help us, but some of them can make us ill if they get inside us. That's not the only threat; you can accidentally swallow very tiny eggs, which—and this is really disgusting—can grow into things like worms that like nowhere better to live than inside your stomach and intestines. Some of them even pop their heads out of your rear at night to lay their eggs!

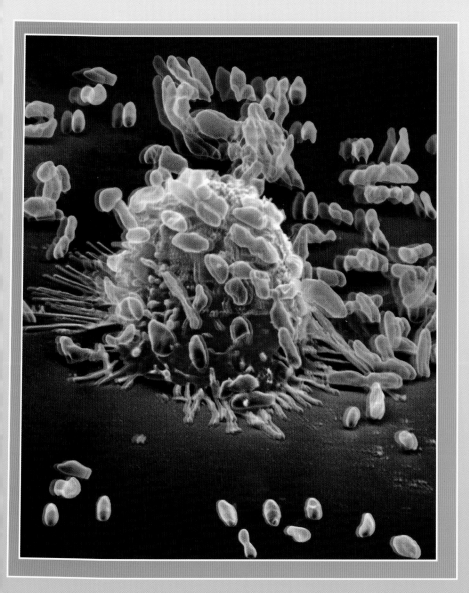

◄ WHITE BLOOD CELLS

Despite all the barriers, harmful bacteria will always get into your body, but then your blood comes into play. Your blood is made up of red and white blood cells. The red cells move the oxygen around your body while the white cells act like security guards. They are on the lookout for harmful bacteria and get rid of them by swallowing them up.

One of the simplest and most effective ways of reducing the risk of bacteria getting into your body is to wash your hands regularly.

LOOKING AFTER NUMBER ONE ►

Although your body is really good at looking after itself, it still needs a helping hand. Basically, the better you look after yourself, the better you'll feel. And it's not difficult. Eating fresh fruit and vegetables gives your body the vitamins it needs to help fight bacteria. Regular exercise gets the lungs and heart working better and pumps the blood through your veins. And getting plenty of sleep helps the brain to organize all your thoughts. A better rested and fitter body is in a better position to tackle diseases, so for the sake of your own well-being, hop to it!

Contributor credits:
3-D glasses illustrator: Ian Thompson
3-D images: Pinsharp 3-D Graphics

Further credits by chapter:

SPACE
Author: Paul Harrison
Picture credits: Corbis; NASA; Science Photo Library.

SOLAR SYSTEM
Author: Marc T. Nobleman
Picture credits: Bruce Coleman/Michael J Howell; Galaxy
Picture Library; Genesis Space Photo Library; NASA; Robert
Harding Picture Library; Science Photo Library.

EXPLORING SPACE
Author: Paul Harrison
Picture credits: Corbis; NASA; Science Photo Library.

JUNGLE
Author: Paul Harrison
Picture credits: FLPA; Jungle Photos; Nature Picture Library;
NHPA; Still Pictures.

OCEANS
Author: Paul Harrison
Picture credits: AKG; Art Archive; Corbis; FLPA; Getty; Kobal
Collection; Nature Picture Library; NHPA; Science Photo
Library.

SEA MONSTERS
Author: Paul Harrison
Picture credits: Bridgeman Art Library; Chris Harvey-Clark;
Natural History Museum; Nature Picture Library; NHPA;
Science Photo Library; Topfoto.

HUMAN BODY
Author: Paul Harrison
Picture credits: Corbis; Getty Images; Nature Picture Library;
Rex Features; Science Photo Library.

Page 3: Corbis.
Page 112: Nature Picture Library.